modifiers

modifiers

A Unique, Compendious Collection of More Than 16,000 English Adjectives Relating to More than 4,000 Common and Technical English Nouns, the Whole Arranged in Alphabetical Order by Noun, with a Complete Index of Adjectives.

Laurence Urdang
Editor

Gale Research Company • Book Tower • Detroit, Michigan 48226

Library of Congress Cataloging in Publication Data

Urdang, Laurence.
 Modifiers : a unique, compendious collection of more
than 16,000 English adjectives relating to more than
4,000 common and technical English nouns, the whole
arranged in alphabetical order by noun, with a complete
index of adjectives.

 Includes index.
 1. English language—Adjective—Glossaries, vocabularies, etc. 2. English language—Noun—Glossaries,
vocabularies, etc. 3. Vocabulary. I. Title.
PE1241.U7 1982   428.1   82-9173
ISBN 0-8103-1195-X   AACR2

Contents

v

Foreword

Nouns in English can often be converted into adjectives by the addition of *-ist, -al, -ar, -ed, -ic, -ical, -itious, -ive, -y, -ish,* and *-ous.* Sometimes a minor change in the base word is required. Here are some examples:

bulb	yields	*bulbar* or *bulbous*
comedy	yields	*comedic*
contrast	yields	*contrastive*
exclusivism	yields	*exclusivist* or *exclusivistic*
excrement	yields	*excrementitious*
fad	yields	*faddish*
fish	yields	*fishy*
flower	yields	*flowered* or *flowery*
grief	yields	*grievous*
nation	yields	*national*
psychology	yields	*psychologic* or *psychological*
table	yields	*tabular*

There are many nouns of English, however, that have no adjectival form that can be created by the addition of a suffix (except *-like, -shaped,* etc.) and for which one must resort to either a somewhat more drastic change in the base word (e.g., *table → tabular*), or, often, an entirely different word. It is to this last category of nouns that the reader's attention is turned, for this book concerns chiefly those. What is the adjectival form for *spear?* Unless you wish to say "spear-shaped," "spearlike," "shaped like a spear," or some other paraphrase, it is difficult to find in a dictionary the word *hastate,* which is merely the adjectival form for *spear.* The disadvantage of using the meaningful suffixal words *-like* or *-shaped* is that they carry specific denotations, whereas a true adjectival ending is purely grammatical and has neither connotation nor denotation: it is usually defined in dictionaries by the formula 'of or pertaining to [the root word],' 'of or relating to [the root word],' and so on.

What do you usually do when you need an adjective for *ear,* for which there is no word "earal" or "earic" or "earate"? What you can now do is look it up in this dictionary and find that its adjectival forms are *aural* and *otic.* Similarly, *mouth* has no modifying form readily available, formed on the same stem, and it may not be easy to remember *stomatal, oral,* or *buccal.*

The purpose of *Modifiers* is to provide the user with the appropriate adjective related to a list of selected common nouns. Technical nouns are listed only in rare instances, because they usually form their associated adjectives by the addition of one of the regular suffixes. Technical adjectives abound, however, and the user of this book must be cautioned, for example, that unless he is being intentionally facetious, using *rhopaloceral* for 'of or pertaining to a butterfly' may not be appropriate.

Although adjectives listed here may generally be construed as meaning 'of, pertaining to, or relating to [the noun listed as the entry word],' that is not always the case: for example, *campaniform* means 'bell-shaped,' as one should be able to determine from the ending, *-(i)form;* however, there are many other things in the world that are or can be 'bell-shaped.' Similarly, **bleeding** in the sense '(uncontrollable) hemophiliac' is quite different from **bleeding** in the sense '(*heraldry*) sanglant.' In some instances gist words are offered in parentheses preceding the adjectival forms, as under **birth** one can find "(~ complication) dystocial," but it is not always possible to codify information so neatly.

Modifiers should be looked upon as an adjunct "index" to the dictionary. Many of the adjectives listed can be found in the 2nd Edition of *Webster's New International Dictionary,* G. & C. Merriam, 1934; others can be found in *-Ologies & -Isms,* Gale Research Company (2nd Edition). As a word of caution, the user should note that dictionaries do not provide much useful information about frequency and appropriateness—essentially, whether or not a word is actually used very often and, if so, in what contexts. For that kind of information there is not, at present, a suitable reference book available. Therefore, the user must be careful to try to determine the level at which a word is customarily used in order to avoid awkwardness of style.

The Style of
Modifiers

1. *Modifiers* consists of a main text and an index. The entry words in the main part of the book are all nouns. There are cases where a word might seem to be an adjective: *blending* or *borrowing,* for instance, could be participles; they are to be understood, however, as gerunds—that is, as nouns. Although the words given within entries are all adjectives, they might be used as nouns: *calliphorid,* for instance, could be understood to mean 'a blowfly'; for the purposes of this book, however, such words are to be understood as adjectives: 'of, pertaining to, related to, or characteristic of a blowfly.'

2. The swung dash ($\sim$) is used to avoid repeating the entry word; thus, under **blindness,** "(blue color $\sim$)" should be read as "(blue color blindness)."

3. A comma is used to separate modifiers that are mere variants [e.g., under **branching** (absence of $\sim$), appear "uniramous, uniramose"].

4. A semicolon is used to separate modifiers that have a different meaning [e.g., under **bright,** appear "fulgent; light; nitid, nitidous," setting off 'fulgent' from 'light' from (both) 'nitid' and 'nitidous,' which are variant forms separated by a comma].

5. The index repeats all of the modifiers in alphabetical order, each with the noun associated with it. Thus, the user who encounters a modifier in context—e.g., *femoral artery* or *inguinal hernia*—can look them up in the index and see, at once, that *femoral* is associated with 'thigh' and *inguinal* with 'groin.'

A

aardvark, edentate; tubulidentate.

aardwolf, protelid.

abalone, haliotoid.

abandonment, jettisonable; lost.

abbess, abbatial.

abbey, abbatial.

abbot, abbatial.

abbreviation, truncated.

abdomen, coeliac; celiac; epigastric; ventral; (large ∼) ventripotent.

abhorrence, disgustful, disgusting.

ability, habile.

abjuration, disclamatory.

abjurement, disclamatory.

abnormality, (*archaic*) exorbitant.

abominability, disgustful, disgusting.

abrasion, discoid.

abrogation, recissible, recissory.

absence, (grammatical ∼) abessive; privative; zero.

absorption, engrossed; inhibitory; porous; saturated; sorbifacient.

abstinence, abstemious; ascetic, ascetical.

abstraction, recondite.

absurdity, farcical; inane; (*rare*) stultiloquent.

abundance, feracious; numerous; plenteous, plentiful, plenty.

abuse, (verbal ∼) vilipendious, vituperative, vituperious.

abyss, bassalian.

accent, (absence of ∼) atonic; emphatic; (between ∼) intertonic.

acceptance, fatalistic.

access, accostable.

accessory, appurtenant.

accident, fortuitous; serendipitous.

acclivity, sloped.

accompaniment, assistance; comitative.

accomplishment, achievable; dispatchful.

account, actuarial.

accumulation, acervuline.

accuracy, veracious.

accusation, invective.

achievement, dispatchful.

acid, acerb, acerbic; acetic, acetose; aliphatic; allanturic; (*obsolete*) esurine.

acknowledgment, admitted.

acorn, balaniferous, balanoid.

acquaintance, familiar.

acquisition, usucaptable, usucaptible.

acronym, acrostic.

acting, dramaturgic, dramaturgical; histrionic, histrionical; Thespian.

action, automatic; disrespectful; (lack of ~) lazy.

activity, abustle; brisk; lish.

acute, smart, smarty.

adage, aphoristic.

adaptation, accommodable, accommodative; adjustable, adjustive; labile; tractable; versative.

addition, accessional; adjunct, adjunctive; adscititious; adventitious; excrescent; summable; supervenient.

address, allocutive; salutational, salutatious, salutiferous.

adhesion, agglutinant, agglutinate, agglutinative; mastic.

adjacency, adjoining; juxtaposed; neighbor, neighbored, neighboring.

adjoinment, adjacent; neighbor, neighbored.

administration, dispensative.

admiration, emulous.

admission, intromissive.

adornment, ornamental, ornamentary, ornate.

adrenal gland, paranephric.

adroitness, nimble.

adult, ephebic.

advance, ahead.

advantage, beneficial.

adventurer, Argonautic.

advice, hortative, hortatory.

advisor, hortative, hortatory.

affectation, afflicted; formal.

affection, fond.

affirmation, asseverative; (*rare*) cataphatic.

affliction, lacerable, lacerant, lacerated, lacerative; pained, painful, paining; vexatious, vexatory.

age, elder, eldest; (old ~) gerastian; geratic, geratologic, geratological; geriatric; gerontic, gerontologic, gerontological; senescent.

aggressiveness, assertative, assertive; somatotonic.

aggression, bellicose; umbrageous.

aging, geratologic, geratological, geratologous; geriatric; gerontologic, gerontological; nostologic; senescent; senile; (fear of ~) gerascophobic.

agitation, discomposed; disgusted; ebullient; nervish, nervous.

agreement, accordant, according; pactional.

agriculture, agrarian, agronomic; campestral; geoponic; georgic.

ague, feverish.

aid, assistant.

air, aeriform; aerologic, aerological; atmospheric; pneumatic; (~ pollution) miasmological; (divination using ~) aeromantic; (dread of ~) aerophobic; (measurement of ~) aerometric.

albatross, procellariiform, procellariid.

alchemy, hermetic, hermetical; spagyric.

alcohol, spiritous; vinic.

alcoholism, bibacious, bibulous; dipsomaniacal.

alder, betulaceous.

ale, (excellence of ∼) nippitate.

alertness, alacrity; brisk; somatotonic.

alfalfa, leguminous.

algae, algological, algous; (∼ eater) algivorous; fucoid, fucoidal, fucous; phycologic.

alien, strange; foreign.

alimentary canal, (absence of ∼) asplanchnic.

alkali, (formation of ∼) kaligenous.

allegory, anagogic.

alleviation, mitigate, mitigated, mitigatory.

alligator, eusuchian; loricate.

allocation, assigned.

allowability, admissible, admissive.

allure, (*obsolete*) illecebrous; sirenic, sirenical.

alphabet, (Arabic ∼) Kufic; (Russian ∼) Cyrillic.

Alps, (north side) transalpine; (south side) cisalpine.

alteration, mutable, mutatory.

altercation, disputant.

alternation of generations, digenetic.

amassing, assemblable.

amazement, agazed; astonished, astonishing; astounding.

amber, succinic, succiniferous.

amberfish, carangid, carangoid.

ambidextrosity, both-handed.

ambience, circumfluent, circumfluous.

ambiguity, Delphic, Delphian; equivocal; oracular; sibyllic, sibylline; tergiversant.

ambush, lochetic.

amendment, repentant; satisfactory.

amplitude, large, largifical.

amusement, madcap.

anaconda, boid; eunectic.

anagram, logogriphic.

anchovy, engraulid.

Andes, Andean, Andine; cisandine.

anemia, chlorotic; exsanguine, exsanguinous; ischemic.

angel, archangelic, archangelical; cherubic, cherubical; seraphic, seraphical.

anger, acerb; acrimonious; (*rare*) excandence, excandescent; fierce; irascent, irate; mad; madcap; maddening, madding, maddish; malevolent; splenetic; umbrageous.

angle, (equal ∼s) isogonal, isogonic.

anglerfish, lophiid.

anguish, dolorific, doloriferous, dolorous; heart-rending; heartsore.

animal, zoic, zooidal, zoologic, zoological; (∼ eater) carnivorous, sarcophagic, sarcophagous, sarcophilous; (∼ form) zoomorphic; (∼ husbandry) zootechnical; (description of ∼s) zoographic, zoographical; (fear of ∼s) zoophobic; (generation of ∼s) zoogenic, zoogonic; (love of ∼s) zoophilic; (wild ∼) feral.

animation, Disneyesque.

ankle, astragalar; talaric.

annal, archival.

annihilation, nihilistic.

announcement, nunciative.

annoyance, bothersome; exasperated; naggish; (*obsolete*) noisome; umbrageous.

annulment, recissible, rescissory.

anointment, aliptic; theochristic.

answer, accountable.

ant, formic, formicine; myrmicine, myrmecoid; (army ~) doryline; (worker ~) ergatomorphic.

antagonist, adversary.

antelope, alcelaphine.

antennae, (absence of ~) acerous; (long ~) dolichocerous; (short ~) brachycerous; (very short ~) microceratous.

anthropoid, pithecan, pithecomorphic.

anticlimax, bathic.

antidote, alexipharmic.

antimony, stibic, stibial.

antiquary, paleophilic.

antiquity, aboriginal; ancient; antediluvian; archaic, archaical, archaistic; paleologic, paleological; (description of antiquities) archaeographical; (devotion to ~) archaeolatrous, philarchaic; (writings of ~) paleographic.

antiseptic, colytic; salicylic.

antler, cervicorn; (deciduous ~) caducicorn.

ant lion, neuropteran, neuropterous.

anus, adanal; proctological, proctologic; (absence of ~) aproctous.

anvil, (~ of the ear) incudate.

anxiousness, eager.

apartness, asunder.

apathy, disinterested; torpid.

ape, pithecan, pithecomorphic; simian, simious.

apex, apicad, apical; cuspidate, cuspidal, cuspate.

aphasia, alalic.

aphid, hemipteroid, hemipterous.

aphorism, apothegmatic, apothegmatical; gnomic; paroemiac; paroemiographical; paroemiological; proverbiological; sententious.

aphrodisiac, venereal.

Aphrodite, Cytherean; Idalian.

Apollo, Paeonian; (festival of ~) Carneian; Delphic; Pythian, Pythic.

apology, deprecatory.

apostate, renegade.

apparition, spectral, spectrological.

appeasement, pacate; pacifiable.

appendage, (absence of ~) exappendiculate.

appetite, edacious; epithumetic; (absence of ~) anorexic, anorectic, anorectous.

apple, maliform; pomaceous, pomiform; (eating ~s) pomivorous.

apportionment, allocable, allocatable; disperse.

approach, adient.

appropriateness, appurtenant; idoneous; (rare) idoneal.

approval, accepted; positive.

aptitude, versatile.

Arabs, Ismaelitic, Ismaelitical, Ismaelitish.

arch, arciform; fornicate, forniciform; (rare) camerated; (subordinate ~) subarcuate.

archery, sagittal, sagittary; toxophilic; (lover of ~) toxophilitic.

architecture, oecodomic, oecodomical.

Arctic, Hyperborean.

ardence, perfervid.

ardor, calentural; vascular.

ardure, hard.
arena, hippodromic.
argument, apagogical; disputatious; dialectic, dialectical; forensic, forensical; perorational, perorative, peroratory; sophistic, sophistical.
aridness, xerothermic.
aristocrat, nobiliary; optimate.
arm, brachial.
armadillo, dasypodid; edentate; loricate; xenarthral.
armor, vambraced.
armpit, axillar, axillant, axillary.
army, (rare) stratonic; stratographic, stratographical; (government by ~) stratocratic.
arrangement, astichous; disponible; systematic.
array, (heraldry) embattled.
arrogance, assumptive; haughty; imperious.
arrow, beloid; sagittal, sagittary; (~ shape) hastate; (divination using ~s) belomantic.
arrowhead, sagittate.
arson, incendiary.
art, abstractionistic.
artichoke, cynaraceous, cynareous, cynaroid.
artificiality, disingenuous.
artificial language, pasigraphic.
artistry, daedal, daedalian.
Aryan, Vedic.
ascension, assurgent.
ascription, assigned.
asexuality, agamic.
ash, cinereous, cineraceous, cineritious, cinerary; (color) cinereal, cinereous.
asparagus, convallariaceous.

asphyxia, apneic, apnoeic.
assembly, auditive, auditory, auditual; conventicular.
assessment, leviable.
assiduousness, painstaking; painsworthy.
assistance, adjutant; available; helpful.
aster, carduaceous.
astringent, kinofluous; (obsolete) pontic; tanniferous.
astrology, Chaldean.
astronomy, Tychonic; uranian, uranological.
Athene, Poliadic.
athlete, mesomorphic.
Atlantic Ocean, cisatlantic; transatlantic.
atmosphere, aerial; airy; aerologic, aerological; nimbused; (divination using ~) aeromantic.
atrocity, dispiteous; flagrant; immane.
atrophy, contabescent.
attachment, adscript, adscripted, adscriptitious, adscriptive; joinable; sessile.
attack, aggressive; (verbal ~) abusive.
attendant, lackeyed; paginal, paginary; yeomanly.
attention, advertent; adviceful; audient; egocentric; urgent; vigilant.
attentiveness, arrect.
attraction, allicient; sirenic, sirenical.
audacity, bodacious; bold.
audience, auditive, auditory, auditual.
auk, charadriiform

austerity, ascetic, ascetical; Catonian, Catonic.

author, auctorial.

authority, cathedral, cathedratic; peremptory; puissant; sceptral.

authorization, aldermanic; legal.

authorship, (false ∼) pseudepigraphic, pseudepigraphical; pseudepigraphal, pseudepigraphous.

avarice, (*archaic*) gripple.

avidness, eager.

avocet, recurvirostrid.

avoidance, abient.

awareness, cognizant; conversant.

awkwardness, gauche.

awl, subulate.

ax, dolabriform.

axis, axial.

B

babbling, stultiloquent, stultiloquious.

baby talk, hypocoristic.

bachelor, celibate; discovert.

back, addorsed; dorsal, dorsiferous; retral; tergal, tergant; ($\sim$ and neck) dorsicollar; ($\sim$ and sides) dorsolateral; ($\sim$ and spine) dorsispinal.

backbone, spinal; rachidiform, rachidial, rachidian.

badger, mustelid.

bag, satcheled.

balance, equilibrious.

baldness, acomous; alopecic; atrichic; calvous; glabrous; (dread of $\sim$) peladophobic.

ball, conglobate.

ballet, choreographic, choregraphical.

balloon, aeronautic, aerostatic.

bandicoot, peramelid, perameline.

bane, pernicious.

banknote, notaphilic.

banter, Aristophanic.

baptism, fontal.

barb, ($\sim$ of a feather) ramal, rameous.

barbering, tonsorial.

barbet, capitonid; piciform.

bargain, pactional.

bark, corticate, corticous, corticiferous, corticiform; ($\sim$ dweller) corticoline, corticolous; epiphloedal, epiphloedic.

barking, hylactic.

barley, alphitomorphous; caryopsid; hordeiform.

barnacle, balanid; cirriped, cirroped; (*rare*) cirripedial; (goose $\sim$) lepadoid.

barracuda, percesocine.

barrel dolioform.

base, (broad $\sim$) platybasic.

baseness, ignoble.

bashfulness, Daphnean; shy; verecund.

basin, pelviform.

basis, fundamental; substrative.

basket, gabioned.

Basque, Euskarian.

bastard, spurious.

bathing, balneal, balneatory; (therapeutic $\sim$) balneological, hydrotherapeutical; (treatise on $\sim$) balneographic.

battle, belliferous, belligerent; Valkyrian.

battlement, castellated.

bay, (color) badius.

beak, rhynchophorous; (deeply cleft ∼) fissirostral; (broad ∼) latinostral; latirostrous; (behind the ∼) opisthodetic; (straight ∼) rectirostral; (upward curved ∼) recurvirostral; (sharp ∼) oxyrhynchous; rhamphoid; rostelliform, rostellate, rostrate, rostrated; rostriferous, rostriform; nebbed.

beam, trabal.

bean, fabaceous, fabiform; leguminiform, leguminose, leguminous; (∼ shape) reniform.

bear, ursine, ursiform.

beard, aristulate; barbate.

bearing, (*heraldry*) bevel.

beast, bestial; theroid.

beauty, aesthetic, esthetic; Aphrodistic; bonny; cosmetic; Junoesque; pulchritudinous; (*obsolete*) venust; (lover of ∼) philocalic.

bedpost, clinoid.

bedroom, cubicular.

bee, allotropous; apiarian, apiological; melittological; (∼ eater) apivorous; (fear of ∼s) apiophobic.

beech tree, cupuliferous.

beekeeping, apiarian.

beestings, (milk) colostral, colostric, colostrous.

beetle, adephagous; coleopteroid, coleopteral, coleopteran, coleopterous; coleopterological; (dung ∼) scarabaeid.

begging, mendicant; precatory.

beginning, early; exordial; inceptive; inchoate, inchoative; incipient; original; primal; principative, principle; tyronic.

behavior, (animal ∼) ethological; (argumentative ∼) litigious, rabulous; (brutal ∼) bestial, brutish, ogreish; (common ∼) plebian; (cowardly ∼) poltroonish; (dissolute ∼) libertine; (foppish ∼) macaronic; (fraudulent ∼) charlatanic; (immature ∼) impubic, puerile; (impractical ∼) quixotic, quixotical; (lewd ∼) pornerastic; (luxurious ∼) Sybaritic; (obsequious ∼) gnathonic, sequacious, sycophantic, toadyish; (officious ∼) polypragmatic; (religious ∼) seraphistic; (risible ∼) gelastic; (roguish ∼) blackguardly; (rowdy ∼) larrikin; (sentimental ∼) maudlin; (stupid ∼) boobyish; (surly ∼) atrabilious; (theatrical ∼) histrionic; (unconventional ∼) bohemian; (whimsical ∼) Shandyesque; (study of ∼) praxeological.

being, ontological.

belch, eructative.

belief, (*obsolete*) credent; doxastic; faithful; opinable, opinative, opiniate, opiniative, opinionable, opinional, opinionate.

bell, caliciform; campaniform, campaniliform, campanological, campanular, campanulate, campanulous, (*rare*) campanarian; jingling; tintinnabulant, tintinnabulary, tintinnabulate, tintinnabulous.

bellflower, campanulaceous.
belligerence, umbrageous.
bellow, mugient.
bell-ringing, tintinnabular, tintinnabulary, tintinnabulous; campanological.
belly, paunched, paunchy; ventral,
ventric, ventricose, ventriculose;
(large ∼) abdominous, ventripotent; (two bellies) biventral,
digastric.
belongings, appurtenant.
beloved, minion.
belt, baldricked.
bend, ajoint; (heraldry) batonic;
bowly; circumflex; curvate,
curvant; reclinate; sinuate, sinuous.
beneficence, bounteous, bountied,
bountiful.
beneficiality, available.
bereavement, viduous.
berry, baccaceous, bacciferous,
bacciform, baccate; (∼ eater)
baccivorous; (producing berries)
cocculiferous.
bestowal, lavish, lavishing.
bet, across-the-board.
betrayal, proditorious; treacherous.
bewilderment, stupefacient, stupefied.
Bible, (destruction of ∼) bib-
lioclastic; (divination from ∼)
bibliomantic; (interpretation of
∼) exegetic.
biceps, bicipital.
bile, (∼ deficiency) acholic; bili-
ary, bilious; cholagogic; (∼ carrier) choledochal; (∼ production)
cholepoietic; choleric, cholic,
cholinic.

birch tree, cupuliferous.
bird, avian; ornithic; ornithologic,
ornithological; volucrine; (∼
eater) avicolous; (∼ egg) oo-
logic, oological; (∼ lover) ornithophilous; (∼ nest) caliological,
nidological; (observation of ∼s)
ornithomantic; (wading ∼s) grallatorial; (young ∼) neossological.
bird of paradise, paradisaeid,
paradisean.
birth, lane-born; naissant; nascent;
natal, natalial; natural; obstetric;
parturient; prenatal; (∼ complication) dystocial; (alien ∼)
aliengenate; congenital; connatal.
birthday, natalitial.
bishop, episcopal.
bite, mordant; morsal; occlusal.
bittern, ardeid.
bitterness, acrimonious; austere;
sardonic; vitriolic.
black bass, centrarchoid.
blackbird, icterine.
black magic, necromantic.
blackness, ebon; jetty; (heraldry)
sable; xanthomelanous.
black pigment, melaniferous.
Black Sea, euxine; Pontic.
bladder, hysterocystic; ultriculi-
form, ultriculoid; urocystic; vesi-
cal, vesicular.
bladderwort, lentibulariaceous.
blade, rapiered.
blame, inculpatory; incriminatory.
blameworthiness, culpable.
blandness, xanthotrichous, xanthous.
bleach, blenching.
bleeding, (heraldry) sanglant; (uncontrollable ∼) hemophiliac.

blend, fondu.
blending, adiagnostic.
blenny, blennioid.
blessing, beatific; benedictory; hallowed.
blind, (window ∼) jalousied.
blindness, ableptical; cecitical; typhlotic; (blue ∼) acyanoblepsic; (blue-yellow ∼) tritanopic; (color ∼) acritochromatic; (day ∼) hemeralopic; (night ∼) nyctalopic; (partial ∼) meropic; (partial color ∼) dyschromatopic; (red-green color ∼) deuteranopic; (snow ∼) chionableptical.
blind spot, scotomatous.
blink, palpebral.
bliss, beatific; Elysian.
blister, aphthoid, aphthous; bullate; pustulant, pustulate, pustular, pustulatous, pustuliform, pustulose; vesicant, vesicate, vesicatory.
blocking, (*archaic*) obstruent.
blood, angiographic, angiographical; (*archaic*) bebled; (*obsolete*) cruent, cruentous; hemal, hematal, haematal, hematic, haematic, hemic; hematologic, hematological; hemoid, hematoid; incruent; sanguinaceous, sanguinary, sanguine, sanguineous, sanguinolent, sanguinous; serologic, serological; (∼ and pus) sanguinopurulent; (∼ circulation) sanguimotor; (∼ drinker) hematophagous, sanguivorous, sanguinivorous; (∼ dweller) hematobic, sanguicolous, sanguinicolous; (∼ poisoning) cachemic, cachaemic; toxemic, toxaemic; (∼ production) hema-

topoietic, haematopoietic; (clot of ∼) grumous; (diseases of the ∼) hemopathological.
bloodlessness, exsanguine, exsanguinous, exsanguious.
bloodsucker, sanguisugous.
bloodthirstiness, carnal; (*obsolete*) sanguisugous.
blood vessel, angioid, angiological, angiopathological; avascular, vascular, vasculolymphatic, vasculose.
blooming, efflorescent.
blossoming, serotinous.
blotch, macular, maculate, maculated.
blowfly, calliphorid.
blueberry, vacciniaceous.
bluebird, turdine.
bluefish, pomatomid.
blueness, azure; cerulean, ceruleous, cerulescent; chalybeous; cyaneous, cyanean, cyanic; lazuline; sapphire, sapphirine.
bluish black, chalybeous; sloe.
bluish gray, cesious.
bluish green, verdazure, verdazurine.
bluish purple, violaceous.
blur, diaphanous.
blush, erubescent.
boa constrictor, boid.
Boadicea, Icenic.
boasting, braggadocian, braggart; (*rare*) jactant; quack.
boat, cymbate, cymbiform; hysteroid; navicular; scaphoid.
bobolink, icterine.
body, corporal, corporeal; somatic, somatologic, somatological; somatosplanchnic; (athletic ∼) mesomorphic; (fat ∼) endomor-

phic, eurysomatic, pyknic; (large ∼) macrosomatous; (slender ∼) asthenic, ectomorphic, leptasomic, leptasomatic; (without a physical ∼) discarnate.

bodyguard, Argyraspidesian.

bog, quaggy.

boil, (infection) furuncular, furunculoid.

boiling, ebullient, ebullitive; fervent.

boisterousness, strepitous, strepitant.

boldness, arrogant, arrogative; saucy; venturous.

bombasticism, lexiphanic.

bone, osseous, ossific, ossiferous; osteographic, osteographical; osteologic, osteological; sclerous; (∼ fracture) agmatological; (between ∼s) interosseous; (disease of the ∼) osteopathic, osteopathological; (divination using ∼s) osteomantic.

bone marrow, myeloid; (∼ destroyer) myelotoxic.

bonhomie, pleasant.

bonnet, mitrate.

booby, (bird) pelecanid, pelecaniform.

book, (∼ hoarding) bibliotaphic; (∼ lover) bibliophilic; (∼ production) bibliogenetic; (∼ theft) bibliokleptomanic; (15th century ∼s) incunabular; (hatred of ∼s) bibliophobic; (history of ∼s) bibliological; (selling of ∼s) bibliopolic; (worship of ∼s) bibliolatrous.

bookbinding, bibliopegic, bibliopegistic, bibliopegistical.

book louse, atropid; psocid, psocine.

bookworm, bibliophagous.

boor, loutish.

boots, ocreated, ocrecite.

border, (*heraldry*) bordured; circumjacent; limbic, limbiferous.

boredom, tedious.

borrowing, acculturational.

bosom, gremial.

botfly, cuterebrid; oestrid.

bottle, aryballoid.

bottom, demersal; (∼ of the sea) bathic.

bottom-dweller, demersal.

bouncing, jouncy.

boundary, (surveying) cadastral; (common ∼) conterminal, conterminate, conterminous; (∼ of dialects) isoglassal.

bounty, lavish, lavishing.

bow, obeisant.

bowerbird, paradisaeid; ptilonorhynchid.

bowlegs, valgoid.

box, locular.

boxing, pugilistic.

braggart, Falstaffian.

braid, lacet.

brain, cerebral, cerebrational, cerebric, cerebriform, cerebroid; encephalic; (∼ convolution) gyral; (lack of ∼) acephalous, acephalic; (smooth ∼) lissencephalic.

branch, cladose; ramiform, ramose, ramous, ramular, ramulose; (between ∼es) interramal; (two ∼es) biramous, biramose.

branching, (absence of ∼) uniramous, uniramose.

brashness, temerarious.

brass, (divination using ~es) chalcomantic.

bravery, bold; valiant, valorous.

brawling, scambling.

breadth, broad; (lack of ~) narrow, narrowy.

break, lacunal, lacunate, lacunary; rhagadiform; (poetic ~) caesuric.

breakfast, jentacular.

breaking, breachy.

bream, cyprinid, cyprinoid.

breast, bosomed; mammary; mammiferous, mammiform; pectoral; subareolar.

breeding, eugenic; (annual ~) monestrous, monoestrous.

brevity, curtal, curtate; ephemeral; short.

brew, poculent.

bribery, venal.

brick, coctile; latericeous, lateritious; samel; (*rare*) samely; sammel.

bridge, cispontine; pontal, pontific; transpontific, transpontine.

brightness, fulgent; light; nitid, nitidous; radiant.

brilliance, bright; lamping; splendent, splendiferous, splenderous; vivid.

brine, brackish; salty.

bristle, chaetiferous, chaetophorous, chaetotactic; echinate; hispid; setal, setaceous, setiform, setulose; spinous, spinose, spinoid.

brittleness, brash; fragile.

bronze, brazen.

brooch, fibular.

brood, (single ~) univoltine.

brother, fraternal; (~ killing) fratricidal.

browbeating, hacked.

brown, (dark ~) brunneous; spadiceous.

Brown, (name) Brunonian.

bruise, ecchymotic; suggillate.

brush, muscariform.

brutality, dispiteous.

bubble, bullate, bulliform; effervescent, effervescive.

buckthorn, rhamnaceous.

budding, gemmate, gemmiparous.

building, architective, architectural; edificable, edificatory, edifical; tectonic; (sacred ~) naological.

bulge, bombé; bulbous; torose; torulose; tuberose, tuberous; tumescent; tumefacient; ventricose.

bulk, large, largifical.

bull, bovine; taurine.

bullfight, tauromachic, tauromachian.

bumblebee, bombid.

bundle, fascicular; (conical ~) fastigiate.

burden, grievous; heavy; laden; onerous; superincumbent.

burglary, (*rare*) kleptistic.

burial, cemeterial; charnel; funeary, funerial; inhumationist; mortuary; sepulchral.

burning, ardent; fervent; (*obsolete*) gledy; calid; comburent, comburivorous; combustible, combustious, combustive; scalded.

burrow, arenicolous; cunicular; effodiant; fossorial.

bush, bosky; dumose, dumous; shock.

buskin, cothurnate.

busyness, assiduous.

butcher, carnificial.
butter, butyraceous.
buttercup, ranunculaceous.
butterfly, lepidopterous, lepidop-
    teral; papilionaceous, papilionid;
    rhopaloceral, rhopalocerous;

(sulphur ∼) pierid.
buttocks, callipygian, callipygous;
    gluteal; natal, natiform;
    steatopygian, steatopygous.
button, knopped, knoppy.
buzzard, cathartine.

C

C, (∼-shape) sigmoid, sigmoidal.
Caesar, Julius, Julian.
calculation, algorismic, algorithmic; tabulated, tabulatory.
calf, vituline.
calling, evocable, evocatory.
callus, porotic; tylotic.
calmness, ataractic; disimpassioned, dispassionate, dispassioned; hesychastic; mild; phlegmatic.
Calvinist, sacramentarian.
Cambridge, Cantabrigian.
camp, castral, castrensian.
cancer, cancroid; cachectic, cachectical, cachexic.
candlelight, lucubratory.
cane, arundinaceous; baculiferous.
cannibalism, androphagous; anthropophagous; thyestean.
cap, calyptrate, calyptriform, calyptrimorphous.
capability, viable.
caper, (∼ plant) capparidaceous.
Cape Town, (So. Africa) Capetonian.
capillary, capillaceous.
Capri, (Italy) Capriote.

capsule, thecal, thecate; vaginiferous.
carbon, anthracoid.
carbuncle, (∼ stone) anthracoid.
cardinal, cardinalic.
carefulness, punctilious.
carelessness, negligent.
carnivore, creophagous; sarcophagal, sarcophagous, sarcophilous.
carp, cyprinid, cyprinoid.
carriage, curricular.
carrion, necrogenic, necrophilous; (∼ eater) necrophagous.
carrying, gestational, gestative; partatile; portable, portative.
cart, plaustral.
cartilage, chondral, chondric, chondroid; endochondral.
carving, anaglyphic, glyptic; xylographic, xylographical, xyloid.
case, capsular, capsuliferous, capsuligerous, capsuliform, capsulogenous.
case history, casuistic.
cashew, anacardic.
castle, castellar, castellate.
castrate, spadonic.

cat, ailuroid; feline; kitling; (fear of ~s) aelurophobic, ailurophobic, elurophobic, felinophobic, gatophobic; (love of ~s) ailurophilic, felinophilic, philofetistic.

catacomb, catacumbal.

catalogue, nomenclatorial, nomenclatural.

Catalonia, Catalan.

caterpillar, eruciform.

catfish, siluroid, silurid.

catharsis, lapactic.

Cathay, (*obsolete*) Cataian.

cathedral, cathedralic.

catkin, cupuliferous.

cattle, bovine.

cause, afflictive; agnogenic; etiologic, etiological; incitant; originary.

causticity, acidulous.

caution, cautelous.

cave, speleological, spelaeological; (~ dweller) cavernicolous, spelaean, spelean, troglodytic.

cavity, carious; coelomate, coelomatic, coelmic; locular; vacuolar.

cedar, (*poetic*) cedarn; cedrine, cedry.

Celebes, Celebesian.

celebration, jubilean.

celebrity, famous.

cell, cellate, cellated, celliform, celloid, cellular, cellulate, cellulose; cytoid; cytologic, cytological; idioplasmatic, idioplasmic; pericytial; phagocytic; trophoplasmatic, trophoplasmic; (~ division) cytodieretic; locular; (~ eater) cytophagous; (~ nucleus) karyologic, karyological; (new ~) epigenetic.

Celts, (Wales) Ordovician.

cement, cementitious.

censure, critical; dyslogistic; illaudable; vituperable, vituperatory.

center, (*rare*) umbilic; (away from the ~) centrifugal; (toward the ~) centripetal.

centipede, scolopendriform.

cerebellum, branial.

ceremony, ritual; sacral, sacramental, sacramentary.

certainty, assured; positive, positivistic; apodictic.

chain, catenarian, catenary, catenate, catenulate, catenoid; (twisted ~) torquated.

chair, cathedral.

chalice, calycine, calycoid.

chalk, cretaceous; (~ drawing) calcographic, calcographical.

chamber, cameral, camerate; locular; vestibular, vestibulate; (single ~) monothalamous, monothecal, unicameral, unilocular; (double ~) bicameral; (two ~s) bilocular.

chamois, rupicaprine.

chance, fortuitous; hazardous; random; (*obsolete*) temerarious; serendipitous.

chancellor, cancellarian.

change, innovatory; labile; metastatic; mutable, mutatory; variable, variant, varied; vicissitous; (color ~) allochroic, allochroous; (~ of mind) flexanimous; (radiant energy ~s) actinic.

changelessness, static.

channel, canalicular, canaliculate, canaliferous; cannelured; lagoonal.

chanting, cantative, cantatory; incantational, incantatory.

chapter, capitular, capitulary; chapitral.

character, (absence of ~) nulliplex; (one's own ~) idiosyncratic, idiosyncratical.

charcoal, anthracoid; carbonous.

charge, accusational, accusatory, accusive; adjuratory.

charity, caritative; eleemosynary; philanthropic.

charivari, callithumpian.

Charles, Carlovingian; Caroline, Carolinian, Carolingian.

chart, cartographic, cartographical.

Charterhouse School, Carthusian.

Chartreuse, Carthusian.

chastity, vestal; virginal; (rare) virgineous; (absence of ~) pornerastic.

chatoyancy, cymophanous.

chatter, babblative, babblesome, babbling; jabbering; jangly; loquacious; yappy.

cheek, buccal; genal; malar.

cheer, (absence of ~) dispiriting.

cheerfulness, eupeptic; jocund.

cheese, caseous; fromological; tyrogenous, tyroid; (divination using ~) tyromantic.

cherry, drupaceous.

Cheshire, Cestrian.

chest, pectoral; thoracic.

Chester, Cestrian.

chewing, masticatory; manducatory.

chicken pox, varicellar, varicelliform, varicelloid.

chickweed, alsinaceous.

chiding, objurgative, objurgatory.

chief, arch; principal; sachemic.

child, youthful, youthly; (~ dentistry) pedodontic; (care of children) pediatric; (fear of children) pedophobic; (hatred of children) misopedic; (killing of children) filicidal.

childbirth, obstetric, obstetrical; parturient, parturitive; puerperal.

childishness, bairnish; puerile.

chill, frigorific; shivering.

chimpanzee, simiid.

chin, verticomental.

China, Sinological.

Chinese, (humorous) Celestial.

chivalry, gallant, galliard; galloptious.

choice, cooptative; elect, elective, electoral, electorial; optative; volitient.

choir, choric.

choir-leader, choragic.

choking, strangulative; (fear of ~) pnigophobic.

chorus, choreutic.

chorus-leader, choragic.

chronicle, archival.

chronology, (~ of earth) geochronologic, geochronological; (comparative ~) synchronological; (error in ~) anachronistic, anachronistical, anachronous, metachronic, parachronic.

church, ecclesial, ecclesiastic, ecclesiastical; ecclesiographic, ecclesiographical; spiritual; (~ building) ecclesiologic, ecclesiological; (Christian ~) ecumenic, ecumenical, oecumenic, oecumenical; (devotion to ~) ecclesiolatrous; (hatred of ~) ecclesiophobic; (opposition to ~) ecclesioclastic.

Church Fathers, patrologic; patrological.

churl, boorish, carlish.

cider, pomaceous.

circle, cingular; circinate; cycloid, cycloidal; ecliptic, ecliptical; gyratory, gyrous; nummiform, nummular; orbic, orbicular; (quarter ∼) quadrant. See also *ring.*

circulation, ventilate, ventilative; (blood ∼) sanguimotor.

circumlocution, periphrastic.

cirrus, cirrate, cirrose, cirrous.

citizen, civic.

city, civil; metropolitan; municipal; oppidan; urban, urbanistic.

civet, viverrid, viverriform, viverrine.

clamminess, sammy.

clamor, boisterous; obstreperous; strepitous, strepitant; vociferant, vociferous.

clan, gentilic.

clarification, analytic; vivificative.

clarity, pellucid.

classification, systematic; taxonomic; (∼ of trivia) micrologic; (botanical ∼) Linnean; (museum ∼) museographic; (soil ∼) agrologic.

claw, chelate, cheliferous, cheliform; unguiculate, unguiferate, ungual, ungular.

clay, argillaceous, argilliferous, argilloid, argillous; figuline; kaolinic; lutaceous.

cleaner, abstergent; smectic.

cleanliness, abstergent, abstersive; hygenic; kosher; neat; (abnormal ∼) ablutomanic.

cleansing, clysmic; lavational, lavatory.

clearness, vivid.

cleavage, archiblastic.

cleaver, dolabriform.

cleft, rimose; (small ∼) rimulose.

clemency, lenient, lenitive.

clergy, cleric, clerical; ecclesiastic, ecclesiastical; vicarial, vicariate.

clerk, scribal; secretarial; clerical.

cleverness, nimble; shrewd; smart, smarty.

click beetle, elaterid.

cliff, bluffy; precipitous.

climbing, scandent, scansorial, scansorious.

clinging, adhament; adherent; adhesional, adhesive.

clique, factional, factionary, factious.

cloak, tabarded.

clock, horologic, horological.

cloister, claustral.

closeness, near; proximate.

closing, occluse; occlusive.

clot, styptical.

cloth, sheety; textile.

clothing, habilable; (*rare*) habilatory; habilimental, habilimented; habited; vestiary.

cloud, duplicatus; foggy; nebulous; nephological; nimbose; noctilucent; nubilous.

cloud cuckoo land, nephelococcygian.

clover, (*heraldry*) trefoiled.

clown, (*obsolete*) lobbish.

club, clavate, clavated, claval; (∼ carrier) claviger.

clumsiness, gauche; maladroit; stogy.

cluster, glomerate.

coal, carboniferous, carbonigerous.

coarseness, boisterous; carlish; harsh; stogy.

coast, lacustral, lacustrine; limicoline; littoral; neritic; ovarian.

cobweb, cortinate.

cockles, cardiacean.

cod, gandid, gandoid.

code, cryptographic; (~ breaking) cryptoanalytic; (writing in ~) cryptogrammic.

coelom, cavitary.

cognizance, sensible.

cohabitation, contubernal, (*obsolete*) contubernial.

coherency, serried.

coil, cirque-couchant; convolute, convolutional, convolutionary; gyrate; helical; tortuous.

coin, numismatic, numismatical; nummary, nummiform.

coincidence, synchronistic, synchronistical.

cold, algid; brumal; cryogenic; frigid, frigorific, frigoric; gelid; hyperborean, hyperboreal; rhigotic; Siberian; (~ blood) poikilothermic, poikilothermous; (~ loving) cryophilic, psychrophilic; (~ hating) psychrophobic; (fear of ~) psychrophobic.

collapse, (*obsolete*) collabent.

collar, (*heraldry*) accollé; torquate.

collecting, (cigar-band ~) brandophilic, cigrinophilic; (coin ~) numismatic; (matchbox ~) cumyxaphilic, philumenic; (stamp ~) philatelic; (air-mail stamp ~) aerophilatelic.

collection, accumulable, accumulate, accumulative; agglomerate, agglomeratic, agglomerative; aggreable, aggregated; assemblable; discographical.

collusion, (*law*) covinous.

color, chromatic; chromatological; hued; idiochromatic; tinctorial; (~ blindness) acritochromatic; (~ printing) chromotypographic; (absence of ~) achromatic; (fear of ~s) chromophobic; (multiple ~s) heterochromatic, heterochromous, limbate, motley, mottled, nacreous, nacred, opalescent; (two ~s) dichromatic.

column, basaltiform, basaltic; systylous.

comb, cteniform.

combination, coadunate; factional, factionary, factious.

comedy, Aristophanic; humorific, humorous; thalian.

command, imperate; jussive; mandative, mandatory; preceptive, preceptory.

commencement, choate, inchoate, inchoative; inceptive.

commerce, Cyllenian.

committing, perpetrable.

commoner, plebian.

commotion, disordered.

community, (unification of communities) synoecious.

compact, pactional.

company, (absence of ~) lonely, lonesome.

comparison, assimilable; dissimilative, dissimilatory.

competence, smart.

complaint, querimonious, querulous, querulent.

completeness, accomplished; (*rare*) choate; plain.

complexion, (white ∼) leucochroic; (dark ∼) melanocomous, melanous, swarthy.

compliancy, (*obsolete*) buxom; manageable; obedient, obediental; obeisant; obsequent, obsequial, obsequious.

complication, Gordian.

composure, disimpassioned, dispassionate, dispassioned.

comprehension, discernible, discerning.

compression, tabloid.

compromise, syncretistic.

computation, arithmetic, arithmetical.

concavity, dished.

concealment, abstraction; celative; delitescent; larvate; perdu, perdue; secret, secretive.

concentration, (∼ on oneself) egoistic, egotistic.

conciliation, irenic, irenical.

conciseness, serried.

conclusion, perorational, perorative, peroratory.

concordancy, harmoniacal, harmonial, harmonic, harmonious.

concubine, hetaeristic, hetairistic.

condemnation, damnatory.

cone, arundiferous, arundinaceous; infundibulate, infundibuliform; strobilaceous.

confidentiality, private.

confinement, (∼ to bed) lectual.

confirmation, verifiable, verificative.

confrere, confraternal.

confusion, atactic; disgusted; jumbled, jumbly; macaronic; stupefacient, stupefied, stupent.

confutation, disprovable.

congeal, frozen.

congregation, assemblable.

conjecture, stochastic.

conjugation, anisogamous.

conjuration, necromantic.

connection, affined; vinicular.

consciousness, sentient.

consecration, blessed; hallowed.

consent, assentaneous.

consequence, ecbatic; ensuant.

consideration, disgracious; habit.

consolation, (*rare*) paramuthetic.

conspiracy, (*law*) covinous.

constancy, incessant.

constellation, asterismal; sidereal; zodiacal.

constitution, disposed; politic, political.

construction, abuilding; edificable, edificatory, edificial; tectonic.

consuming, eatable; edible.

consumption, (disease) phthisic, phthisical, tubercular, tuberculous.

contact, attingent.

container, aerohydrous; receptacular.

contamination, septic.

contemporary, coeval; coetaneous, coaetaneous.

contempt, contumelious.

contention, disputant.

contentment, satisfying.

contestant, agonistic, agonistical.

contestation, disputable, disputatious.

continuation, perennial.

contortion, tortuous; wried, writhen.

contraction, systaltic, systolic.
contradiction, antinomic, antinomian.
contrast, dissimilative, dissimilatory.
contribution, accessory; adjuvant.
control, manageable; epistatic.
controversy, disputant; eristic, eristical; philopolemic.
convalescence, anastatic.
convenience, gain; handy.
convergence, centrolineal.
conversation, confabular, confabulatory; deipnosophistic; sophistical.
conveyance, afferent; kinesodic; verbal.
convolution, cerebriform.
convulsion, clonic.
cookery, culinary; cuisinary; kitchen; magiric.
cooling, algefacient; refrigerative; frigorific, frigiferous; frigoric.
coolness, disimpassioned, dispassionate, dispassioned.
cooperation, coadjuvant; synergic.
coordination, eupractic.
copiousness, fluent.
copper, cupreous, cuprous, cupric; chalcographic, chalcolithic.
copy, apographal; facsimile.
coral, madreporian, madreporic.
cord, restiform.
cork, suberose, subereous, suberic.
cormorant, phalacrocoracine.
corner, angulous; nooklike.
corona, leucospheric.
corporeality, bodily.
corpse, cadaverous, cadaveric; (dissection of ~s) necrotomic; (feeding on ~s) necrophagous; (love of ~s) necrophilic; (worship of ~s) necrolatrous.
correction, emendatory.
correctness, just.
correspondence, same; epistolary, epistolic; epistographic.
corrosion, caustic, caustical.
corruption, adulterate, adulterant, adulterine; evil; flagitious; reprobate; venal.
corundum, sapphire, sapphiric.
costliness, precious.
cotton, byssoid.
cough, tussal, tussic, tussive.
count, comital; numerable, numerant, numerative.
counterfeit, fake.
country, (one's own ~) domestic.
courage, brave; dauntless; fortitudinous; heroic; intrepid; mettlesome; valiant, valorous.
course, curricular; cursive.
court, (*obsolete*) curial.
cover, acrolithic; obtect, obtected; tegminal; integumentary.
cow, bovine.
coward, caitiff; craven; lily-livered; pusillanimous; recreant.
cowl, capistrate; cucullate.
cowrie, cypraeiform, cypraeid, cypraeoid.
crack, rhagadiform; rimose, rimous; rimulose; shaky.
crackle, cremant; crepitant.
craft, colubrine.
craftiness, (*archaic*) cautelous.
cramp, idiospastic.
cranberry, vacciniaceous.
crane, (bird) grallatorial.
crane fly, tipulid, tipuloid.
crank, pagurian.

crawling, reptatorial, reptant.

creaking, stridulant, stridulent, stridulous.

creation, poietic.

creativity, (*rare*) gignitive; poietic.

credibility, authentic.

creosote, cresylic.

crescent, bicorn; demilune; lunate, lunular, lunulate.

crest, cristate, cristiform; pileate.

crevice, rimose, rimous; vallecular, valleculate.

crime, flagitious; (relapsing into ∼) recidivistic, recidivous.

criminal, flagitious; malfeasant; delose; (*archaic*) nocent.

criticism, calumnious; captious; censorious; illaudatory; objurgatory; scurrilous; Zoilean.

cross, chiasmal, chiasmic; cruciate, cruciform, crucificial, cruciferous, crucigerous; decussate, decussated.

crossroads, compital; quadrivial.

crowd, coacervate; gregal, gregarian, gregarious; populous; serried; (fear of ∼s) agoraphobic, demophobic, ochlophobic; (fondness for ∼s) demophilic; (hatred of ∼s) demophobic.

crown, coronal, coronary, coronated; (∼ shape) coroniform.

crudeness, kutcha.

cruelty, barbaric, barbarous; brutal, brutish; cannibalic; dispiteous; fiendish; fierce; sadic, sadistic.

crustacean, (∼ eater) cancrivorous.

cucumber, cucumiform; cucurbitaceous.

culpability, guilty.

cultivation, agricultural; educable, educatable; (absence of ∼) fallow.

cultivator, laetic.

culture, (anthropology) ethnic, ethnologic, ethnological; (lack of ∼) Philistine; vulgar.

Cumberland, Cumbrian.

cunning, colubrine; shrewd; subdolous.

cup, acetabular; cyathiform; cyphellate; pezizaeform, peziziform, pezizoid; (*rare*) pocilliform; poculiform; scyphate, scyphiform.

cure, sanable, sanative, sanatory; treacly.

curl, crispate; crisp.

curlicue, scriggly.

current affairs, topical.

curse, execratory; imprecatory; maledictory.

curtsy, obeisant.

curve, arciform; arcual, arcuate; bandy; falcated; flexuous; gyrate; (*heraldry*) nowy; obvolent; sinuate, sinuous.

cushion, paddy; pulvinate.

custodian, Cerberean, Cerberic; janitorial.

custom, consuetudinal, consuetudinary; formal; habitual, habituate; national; nomic.

cutting, satiric, satirical; incisal, incisory, incisorial, incisive; severable, severed; sharp; (plant ∼) sarmentose.

cuttlefish, sepiid.

cynicism, misanthropic.

cypress, cyprine.

cyst, hydatiform.

D

dallying, desipient.
damage, disserviceable.
dampness, rafty.
damselfish, pomacentrid.
damselfly, coenagriidaeceous; odonate.
dance, balletic; choreographic; orchestric; saltatory, saltatorial, terpsichoreal, terpsichorean.
danger, adventurous, adventuresome; jeopardous; parlous; periculous; seathy.
daring, venturous.
darkening, obumbrate.
darkness, acheronian, acherontic; caliginous; Cimmerian; dispirited; ebon, ebony; nigritudinous; (*rare*) opacous; tenebrous; (fear of ∼) nyctophobic, scotophobic.
dart, (∼ shape) belemnoid.
daughter, filial.
dauntlessness, bold.
dawn, auroral, aurorean; eoan.
day, diurnal; quotidian; (∼ and night) noctidiurnal, nychthemeral; (∼ blindness) hemeralopic.
daze, astonished; stupefacient, stupefied.

deacon, diaconal.
deafness, anacusic.
dean, decanal.
death, agonal; defunct, defunctive; feral; fatal; funest; lethal, lethiferous; necrotic; (*rare*) nerterological; obequial; obitual, obituary; posthumous; postmortem; Thanatotic; thanatological; (announcement of ∼) necrologistic; (divination involving ∼) necromantic; (fear of ∼) necrophobic, thanatophobic; (feigning ∼) necromorphous; (resembling ∼) thanatoid.
debasement, adulterant, adulterate.
debate, discussive; forensic; quodlibetic.
debilitation, asthenic.
debris, detrital.
debruising, (*heraldry*) oppressed.
debt, funded.
decapitation, acephalic, acephalous.
decay, carious; disintegrable; marcid; saprogenic, saprogenous, sapropelic.

deceit, cautelous; covinous; gnathonic; hypocritical; illusive, illusory; imposterous, impostrous; Janusfaced, Januslike.

deception, disingenuous; fallacious, fallible; perfidious; obreptitious; sirenic, sirenical.

decision, arbitral; decretory; judicial, judicious.

declination, sloped.

decomposition, disintegrable; photolytic; rancid.

decoration, adorned; fangled; ornamental, ornamentary, ornate.

decree, decretorial, decretory; edictal; sanctionary, sanctionative.

deer, artiodactylous; cervine, cervid; venison; (red ~) elaphine; (roe ~) capreoline.

deerfly, tabanid.

defamation, aspersive; obloquial, obloquious.

defeatism, futilitarian.

defect, lacunate, lacunal, lacunary.

defender, advocatory.

deference, obeisant.

deficiency, (~ of bile) acholic; (~ of moisture) xeric; (mental ~) oligophrenic.

deftness, handy.

degeneration, autolytic; cacogenic.

degradation, infranatural.

degree, gradal.

dehydration, desiccant.

deity, holy.

dejection, disheartening; dismal; dispirited.

delay, dilatory; hesitant, hesitative, hesitatory.

delegate, vicarial.

delicacy, fragile.

delineation, graphic.

Delphi, pythic, pythian.

deluge, diluvial.

delusion, hallucinational, hallucinative, hallucinatory.

demigod, daemonic, daimonic.

demon, cacodemonic, caecodemonic, cacodemoniac, caecodemoniac; (fear of ~s) bogyphobic.

denial, atheistic; dismissive; negative; nihilistic.

Denmark, Danic, Danish.

density, turbid; (equal ~) isopycnic.

denunciation, comminative, comminatory; invective; objurgatory; obloquious.

departure, valedictory; apopemptic.

dependence, reliant.

dependency, anaclitic; parasitic; symbiotic.

depravity, cankered.

depression, disheartening; dismal; dispirited; oblate; sad; glenoid.

deprivation, discredited; dispossessed.

depth, bathyalic, bathyal; (~ of water) bathymetric, bathymetrical; (*obsolete*) neal; (lack of ~) ebb; shallow; shoal.

deputy, legative; nabobical; vicarial; delegatory.

Descartes, Cartesian.

descent, (*astrology*) cadent.

description, adjectival; delineative.

desecration, sacrilegious.

desert, eremological; (hermit in ~) eremitic; (~ dweller) eremophilous, xerophilous; (fear of ~) xerophobic.

desertion, tergiversant, tergiversatory.

designation, assigned; name; nomenclatural.

desire, cathectic; eager; epithumetic; erogenous; (sexual ~) aphrodisiac, nymphomaniacal.

desolation, sole; solitary.

despondency, disconsolate.

destitution, (*obsolete*) nace; naughty.

destruction, internecine, internecive; vandalish, vandalistic.

detachment, discerptible, discretive, disjoinable.

detergent, abstergent.

deterioration, (~ of race) dysgenic.

determinism, fatalistic, karmic.

detonation, fulminant.

development, accelerated; educable, educatable; (excessive ~) hypertrophic; (inadequate ~) hypotrophic.

deviation, eccentric, eccentrical.

devil, cacodemoniac, cacodaemoniac; caecodemonic, cacodaemonic; cacodemonial, cacodaemonial; diabolic, diabolical, diabological; Luciferian; satanic; (worship of ~) diabolistic.

devotion, addicted; assiduous; ritual; votal, votary, votive; wholehearted; whole-souled.

devouring, eatable; edible; (*heraldry*) vorant.

dew, (*rare*) roral; roric; (*obsolete*) rorid; (*rare*) roscid; (*rare*) roriferous; (*rare*) rorifluent.

dexterity, adroit.

diagram, graphic; schematic.

dialogue, interlocutory.

diamond, adamantine; diamantine, diamantiferous; vajra.

diaphragm, phrenic.

dicast, heliastic.

diction, (poor ~) cacological.

dictionary, lexicographic, lexicographical, lexigraphic; nomenclatorial, nomenclatural.

didacticism, (*archaic*) didascalic; tendentious.

difference, dissimulative, dissimilatory; heterologous.

difficulty, Gordian; hard; scabrous.

diffidence, shamefaced, shamefast, shameful; shy.

digestion, acidoprotelyctic; (bad ~) cacograstric, dyspeptic; (good ~) eupeptic; peptic.

digging, (*rare*) excavate; excavational, excavatorial; fossorial.

digit, dactylic, dactylar; (five ~s) pendactylate, pendactylic; (flat ~s) platydactylous.

dignity, (highest ~) curule.

digressiveness, discursive.

dilatation, systaltic; variciform, varicoid, varicosity.

dilation, ampulliform.

dilatoriness, procrastinating, procrastinatory, procrastinative.

diligence, assiduous; eident; operose; painstaking; painsworthy.

diluent, humectant.

dimension, scantlinged.

dimness, crepuscular; opacous.

dinginess, subfusc, subfuscous.

dining, (*rare*) aristological; deinodiplomatic; (fear of ~) deipnophobic.

dining hall, refectorian, refectorarian, refectorial.

dinner, prandial.

dinosaur, diapsidan.

diplomacy, fetial, fecial.

dirge, epicedial, epicedian; threnetic; threnodial, threnodian, threnodic, threnodical.

dirt, colluvial; (fear of ~) misophobic, musophobic, mysophobic; (love of ~) mysophilic.

disability, lame, lamish.

disaccord, disconformable, disconsonant.

disagreement, disconformable, disconsonant; discrepant; dissentient, dissentious; dissident.

disappearance, effaceable; vanishing.

disapproval, deprecative, deprecatory; dyslogistic.

disarray, disheveled.

disassembly, clastic.

disbelief, atheistic; nullifidian.

discard, repudiable.

discernment, discoverable; perceiving.

discharge, efferent; effluent.

decisiveness, peremptory.

discomfort, dysphoric.

disconnection, discerptible; discretive; disjoinable.

discontent, dissatisfied.

discord, absonant; adjar; dissentaneous.

discordance, cacophonic, cacophonical, cacophonous.

discouragement, disheartening; dismal.

discourse, narratable, narrative, narratory; perorational, perorative, peroratory; sermonic.

discovery, heuristic.

discretion, arbitrable; arbitrary.

discussion, dissertational, dissertative.

disdain, contumelious; haughty; scornful; snobbish.

disease, allotrylic; morbid, morbiferal; morbiferous, morbific; nosologic, nosological; plaguy; sick, sickish, sickly; (bearing ~) pestiferous; (contagious ~) zymotic; (fear of ~) nosophobic, pathophobic; (termination of a ~) lytic, lyterian.

disgrace, obloquious; scandalous; scarlet.

disguise, veiled.

disgust, nasty; nefandous; noisome.

disheartenment, discouraging.

dishonor, obloquious.

disinclination, adverse.

disintegration, atmoclastic; calcinatory; karyoclastic.

disjunction, discerptible; discretive; disjoinable.

disk, (~ -shaped foot) discopodous; nummular.

dislike, antipathic; (~ of crowds) demophobic; (~ of gold) aurophobic; (~ of odors) osphresiophobic; (~ of saints) hagiophobic; (~ of wealth) chrematophobic; (~ of wood) hylephobic; (~ of writing) graphophobic.

dislocation, diastasic; disjointed; disoriented.

disloyalty, (obsolete) disleal.

dismissal, dischargeable; dismissory.

disobedience, contumacious; recalcitrant; refractory; wayward.

disorder, disgusted; farraginous; (mental ∼) paranoiac; rabble; raffish; slovenly; (fear of ∼) ataxiophobic, ataxophobic.

dispensation, administerial, administrable.

dispersion, scatter, scattered, scattering.

displacement, disoriented; (*heraldry*) fracted.

displeasure, dissatisfied; umbrageous.

dispute, arguable, argumental; eristic; litigious.

disquiet, discomposed.

disruption, cataclysmic.

dissection, vivisective.

dissemblance, Aesopian; dissimulative.

dissent, disconformable, disconsonant; factious; recusant.

dissimilarity, difform.

dissolution, (∼ of stone) saxifragous.

dissolving, resolvent, solvent.

dissonance, cacophonic, cacophonous; disconformable; disconsonant.

distaste, antipathetic.

distinction, discrete, discretive; discriminable, discriminant, discriminative.

distinguishability, articulate, articulative.

distortion, anamorphous.

distress, aggrieved.

disturbance, discomposed; disgusted; upset.

disuse, desuetudinous.

ditch, fossorial.

diurnality, journalary.

diversification, variate, variational, variative; varied; varietal; various.

diversion, wried.

diversity, (∼ of color) varicolored, varicolorous.

divination, mantic; (∼ by crystal ball) gastromantic; (∼ by bones) osteomantic; (∼ by wood) xylomantic; (false ∼) pseudomantic.

division, discerptible, discretive, disjoinable; dissectional, dissective; fissiparous; mitotic; schismatic, schismatical, schismic.

divisor, aliquot.

divorcee, discovert.

dizziness, scotomic.

doctor, iatric (fear of ∼s) iatrophobic.

dodo, columbiform.

dog, canine; cynic, cynoid; (∼ face) cynocephalous, cynocephalic; (dread of ∼s) cynophobic; (love of ∼s) philocynical.

dogfish, squaloid.

Dog Star, cynic, Sothic.

dogwood, cornaceous.

dolefulness, funest.

dollarfish, stromateoid.

dolphin, cetacean, cetaceous; delphine, delphinoid.

domestication, tame.

domicile, homish.

dominance, hegemonic; imperious.

donkey, cardophagous.

dormancy, latent, latescent.

dormouse, myoxine.

dose, posologic, posological.

dot, punctate, punctiform, punctuate, punctulate.

double, diploid; geminate.

doubt, dubious; juberous.

doughnut, (∼ shape) toric, toroid.

dove, columbiform; columbine.

down, lanuginous; mollipilose, mollitious; nappy; pappose; puberulent; sericated; tomentose.

dowsing, rhabdomantic.

drabness, subfusc, subfuscous.

dragon, draconic.

dragonfly, libellulid; odonate.

drama, theatral; thespian.

drawing, diagraphical; graphic; (∼ with chalk) chalcographic; (∼ maps) planographic, planographical; (∼ in perspective) scenographic, scenographical; (shadow ∼) skiagraphical.

dream, hallucinational, hallucinatory; oneiric; somnial; visionary; (divination using ∼s) oneiromantic; (interpretation of ∼s) oneirocritical.

dreariness, dismal; Novemberish.

dregs, colluvial.

drink, potable.

drinking, bibitory, bibulous; potatory; (excessive ∼) crapulous; (fear of ∼) dipsophobic.

drooping, cernuous.

drop, guttate; stilliform.

droplet, guttiform, guttular, guttulate.

dropsy, anasarcous.

dross, recrementitious; scoriac, scoriaceous, scoriform.

drought, (sensitivity to ∼) xerophobic, xerophobous; (tolerance for ∼) xerophilic, xerophilous.

drowsiness, lethargic; oscitant; torpid.

drug, pharmacognostic; pharmacological; (addiction to ∼s) toxicomaniacal; (desire for ∼s) narcomaniacal; (fear of ∼s) pharmacophobic.

drum, tympanic.

drumhead, tympanic.

drumstick, plectridial.

drunkenness, bacchanalian; crapulent; inebriate.

dryness, arid; dessicant; droughty, drouthy; sec; siccative; xeric, xerotic; (fear of ∼) xerophobic.

dry rot, fusarial.

duality, Jekyll-and-Hyde; schizoid, schizophrenic.

duck, anseriform.

duckweed, lemnaceous.

duct, vasiferous, vasiform.

duke, ducal.

dullness, blunt, bluntish; jejune; pedestrian; torpid; vapid; wearisome.

dung, (∼ dweller) fimicolous; stercoraceous.

duplication, (chromosome ∼) disomic.

dura mater, (inside the ∼) intradural.

dusk, subfuscous.

duskiness, phaeochrous.

dust, pruinous, pruinose, pruinate; pulverulent.

dwarf, nanitic, nanoid.

dwelling, arvicoline; domiciliary.

dye, tinctorial.

dyspepsia, cacogastric.

E

eagerness, zealous.

eagle, accipitrid; aquiline.

ear, acousticolateral; aural, auric, auricular; aurous; entotic; otologic, otological; otic; (∼ and nose) aurinasal, otorhinal; (affecting both ∼s) binaural; diotic; (diseases of the ∼) otiatric; (inflammation of the ∼) otitic.

earache, otalgic.

eardrum, tympanic.

earl, comital.

earnestness, serious.

earth, geologic, geological; intratelluric; tellural, tellurian, telluric; (∼ and moon) geoselenic; (∼ eating) geophagous; (crust of ∼) tectonic; (divination using ∼) geomantic; (formation of ∼) geogonic; (surface of ∼) geomorphologic, geomorphological.

earthquake, seismic, seismologic, seismological (equal ∼ shock) isoseismic; (major ∼) macroseismic; (measuring of ∼s) seismographic, seismographical; (minor ∼) microseismic; (violent ∼) megaseismic.

earthworm, lumbricoid, lumbricid, lumbriciform.

earwax, ceruminous, cerumiferous, ceruminiparous.

earwig, forficulid.

ease, affable; effortless; simple.

east, oriental.

Easter, Paschal.

eating, edacious; (∼ any food) omnivorous, pantophagous, polyphagous; (∼ apples) pomivorous; (∼ one food) monophagous; (∼ algae) algivorous; (∼ berries) baccivorous; (∼ carrion) necrophagous; (∼ crustaceans) cancrivorous; (∼ earth) geophagous; (∼ eggs) oophagous; (∼ excrement) scatophagous; (∼ fish) ichthyophagian; (∼ flesh) creophagous, omophagous; (∼ fruit) carpophagous, fructivorous, frugivorous; (∼ grain) granivorous; (∼ grass) graminivorous; (∼ horsemeat) hippophagous; (∼ mollusks) molluscivorous; (∼ mushrooms) mycophagous; (∼ organic waste) detritivorous; (∼ oysters) ostrephagous; (~ plants) herbivorous, phytivorous, phytophagous; (~ rice) oryzivorous; (~roots) rhizophagous; (~ seaweed) fuciphagous; (~ seeds) granivorous, seminivorous; (~ snakes) ophiophagous; (~ tissue) histophagous; (~ trees) dendrophagous; (~ wood) hylophagous, xylophagous; (excessive ~) crapulous; (fear of ~) phagophobic; (good ~) gastronomic, gastronomical.

ebb, refluent, reflux.

echidna, monotremal, monotrematous, monotremous; tachyglossid, tachyglossal, tachyglossate.

echo, (*rare*) catacoustic; cataphonic; onomatopoetic; (*obsolete*) phonocamptic; reboant; reverberant, reverberative.

edema, anasarcous; ascitic.

edge, keen; sharp; vorpal; (notched ~) emarginate, crevelated; (two ~s) ancipital.

editor, redactorial.

editorial, journalistic.

Edom, Idumaean, Idumean.

eel, anguilliform.

eeriness, eldritch, eldrich, elritch.

effervescence, ebullient, ebullitive.

efficiency, (*archaic*) perficient.

effort, labored, laborious, laborsome; operose.

effulgence, bright; brilliant; nitid.

effusion, scaturient.

effusiveness, bubbling; gushing.

egg, ovarious, ovate, ovoid, ovoidal; ovular, ovulate; (~ eater) oophagous; (~ yolk) vitelline.

eggplant, solanaceous.

eight, octad, octadic; octal; octamerous; octuple, octuplet; octuplicate; octuplex.

ejection, ejaculative.

elbow, anconoid; olecranal, olecranial, olecranioid.

election, cooptative.

electricity, galvanic; voltaic.

elegance, (*archaic*) venust.

elegy, epicedial, epicedian; threnodial, threnodic.

elephant, pachydermatous, pachydermous, pachydermic, pachydermal; pachydermoid, pachydermatoid.

elevation, colliculate; elated, elative; umbonic.

elk, cervid, cervine.

elm tree, ulmaceous.

eloquence, dithyrambic; facund.

emaciation, marantic, marasmic, marasmous.

embossment, anaglyphic; empaistic.

embryo, germinal.

emerald, smaragdine.

emetic, anacathartic; nauseous.

emission, secretional, secretionary, secretitious.

emollient, malactic.

emotion, affectional, affectionate, affectionated; affective, affectuous; passional, passionate; pathetic, pathetical; pathognomic; nympholeptic.

emperor, imperatorial.

empiricity, Aristotelian.

emptiness, vacant, vacuous.

emu, ratite.

enaction, disciplinary.

enameling, basse-taille.

enchantment, Circean, Circaean; magical; necromantic; sortilegic, sortilegious.

enclosure, circumvallate; integumentary.

encouragement, hortatory, hortative; protreptic.

end, autotelic; desinent; teleologic, teleological; vergent.

endeavor, conative.

endurance, perseverant.

energy, hearty; sthenic.

engagement, busy.

England, Anglican; (love of ∼) Anglophilic; (fear of ∼) Anglophobic.

engraving, glyptic; graphic; (∼ on gems) dactyliographic, glyptic, glyptographic, glyptological, lithoglyptic, lapidarian; (∼ on steel) siderographic, siderographical; (∼ on wax) cerographic; (∼ on wood) acrographic, acrographical, xylographic, xylographical.

enjoyment, apolaustic; zestful.

enlargement, acromegalic, acromegaloid; ampliate; dilatate, dilatable; dilative; varicose, varicosed, varicosity.

ennui, boring, borish.

ensign, vexillary.

enslavement, (∼ of an ant colony) dulotic.

enthusiasm, ebullient; fanatic, fanatical; nympholeptic.

enticement, alluring.

entirety, all; perfect; plain.

entrails, splanchnic.

entrance, accessible; ingressive.

entreaty, impetrative, impetratory; precatory.

entwinement, braided.

environment, ambient; ecological.

ephemerality, brief.

epicure, Apician.

epidemic, phorological.

epithet, antonomastic, antonomastical.

equality, adequate, adequative; egalitarian, (obsolete) egal; isopycnic; (∼ of depth) isobathyal, isobathic; (∼ of duration) isochronous; (∼ of force) isodynamic; (legal ∼) isonymic; (∼ of pressure) isostatic; (∼ of rainfall) isohyetal; (∼ of temperature) isothermal.

equanimity, disimpassioned, dispassionate, dispassioned.

equivalence, tantamount.

equivocation, jesuitic; parisological.

erasure, effaceable.

erection, priapismic.

erotica, Paphian; Sapphic.

erring, astray.

error, fallacious, fallible; labile; solecistic, solecistical; (fear of ∼) hamartophobic.

eruption, Pelean.

escort, beauish.

Eskimo, Hyperborean.

esophagus, epicardial.

essentiality, necessary.

establishment, accomplished.

estate, alodial; allodial, alodian, allodian; demesnial.

esteem, valued.

estrangement, alienable.

eternity, aeonian; sempiternal; (obsolete) eviternal.

ethics, axiological; deontological; moral.

Ethiopia, Abyssinian.

ethylene, olefiant.

eunuch, spadonic.

Eustachian tube, salpingian.

evaluation, fact-finding; ponderable.

evasion, saponaceous.

evening, nocturnal; vesperal, vesperian, vespertinal.

evergreen, eucryphiaceous; sempervirent, sempervirid.

everything, pantologic, pantological.

evil, bad, baddish; base; flagitious; malefactory; malefic, maleficent, maleficial, maleficiate, malevolent, malevolous; malicious, maliferous; malignant; nefast; ominous; pernicious; (*obsolete*) qued, quede.

evolution, (slow ∼) bradytelic; (backwards ∼) catagenetic.

exaggeration, hyperbolic.

examination, disquisitional, disquisative, disquisitory, disquisitorial; scrutable, scrutinous.

excavation, cavate.

excellence, (*obsolete*) eximious; galloptious.

exception, excipient.

excess, exorbitant; nimious; plethoric; superfluous; surfeited.

exchange, cambial; catalactic.

excitement, agitable; hectic, hectical; nervish, nervous.

exclusion, secluded, seclusive.

excrement, feculent; scatologic, scatological; (eating ∼) scatophagous; (fear of ∼) scatophobic; (love of ∼) coprophilic.

excretion, eccritic; emunctory.

excuse, apologetic; venial.

executioner, carnificial.

exercise, calisthenic; gestatory; gymnastic.

exertion, (lack of ∼) lazy, torpid.

Exeter, Exonian.

exhalation, transpirative, transpiratory.

exhaustion, haggard; jaded; (fear of ∼) kopophobic, ponophobic.

exhibition, ostensible, ostensive; pageant, pageanted, pageanic; scenic.

existence, actual; aged; ontic; ontologic, ontological, ontologistic.

exit, egressive.

exorbitance, disordinate; excessive.

expansion, elastic.

expelling, ejaculative; expulsatory, expulsive.

expenditure, sumptuary.

experience, empirical.

experiment, peirastic.

expertise, habile.

explanation, accountable; exegetic; expositional.

explosion, fulminant.

expression, juratory; neophrastic; peremptory.

expulsion, ejaculative; extrusive, extrusory.

extension, prolate.

exterior, ectal; exoteric.

extermination, genocidal.

externality, extrinsic.

extra, excrescent.

extract, pericopal, pericopic.

extraction, elicitable, elicitory.

extravagance, disordinate; dispendious; excessive; garish; lavish, lavishing; nimious; (*rare*) profluvious; sumptuary.

extremism, Jacobinic; ultraistic.

extremities, acroteric.

extremity, disordinate; excessive; ultra; uttermost.

exultation, elated, elative.

eye, ocellar, ocellated; ocular; ophthalmologic, ophthalmological; optic, optical; (behind the ∼) retroocular; (compound ∼) ommateal, schizochroal; (cross ∼s) esotropic, strabismic; (fear of ∼s) ommatophobic; (large ∼) megalopic; (one ∼) monocular, monoptic; (wall ∼s) exotropic, strabismic.

eyeball, (∼ covering) scleral, sclerotic.

eyebrow, superciliary.

eyelash, ciliary, ciliate.

eyelid, blepharal; palpebral, palpebrate.

eyestalk, stipiform, stipital.

F

fable, Aesopic, Aesopian; fabular,
fabulous.
fabric, textile.
face, facial; janiform; prosopic;
physiognomic; visaged; (broad
~) platyopic; (short ~)
brachyfacial, chamaeprosopic;
(long ~) dolichofacial; (description of ~s) prosographic; (divination using ~s) metopomantic.
facility, easy; fluent; fluid, fluidal;
versatile.
failure, (fear of ~) kakorrhaphiophobic.
faintness, (archaic) evanid.
fair, nundinal.
fairy, elfin, elfish.
faith, believable; fideistic; pistic,
pistological; (lack of ~) disillu-
sionary.
falcon, raptorial.
fall, autumnal.
fallacy, sophistic, sophistical.
Fallopian tube, salpingian; tubate.
fallowness, lea.
falseness, adulterant, adulterate;
disingenuous; fraudulent; spe-
cious; spurious.

familiarity, versed.
family, akin; domestic.
fanaticism, zealotic.
farce, inane.
farewell, apopemtic; valedictory.
farm, villatic.
farmer, agrarian.
farming, agrarian; campestral.
farsightedness, hypermetropic;
hyperopic; presbyopic, presbytic.
fascination, sirenic, sirenical.
fashion, à la mode; au courant.
fastidiousness, finical; nice.
fat, adipose, adipogenetic; corpu-
lent; lardaceous; liparoid,
liparous, lipogenous, lipoid; pinguid; sebaceous; sebific; stearic;
stout; (producing ~) sebiferous.
fatality, lethal; mortiferous, mor-
tuous.
fate, karmic; kismetic.
father, paternal; patriarchal, patriarchic, patriarchical; patriclinous;
patristic, patristical; (derived
from ~'s name) patronymic;
(hatred of ~) misopateristic;
(killing of ~) parricidal, patri-

cidal; (related through ∼) patrilateral.
fatigue, languent, languescent, languid, languishing; lethargic.
fault, vitiate.
faultfinding, captious.
favor, advantageous; disgracious;
privileged.
favoritism, partisan; (∼ to rela-
tives) nepotic, nepotistical, (*rare*)
nepotious.
fear, aghast; pavid; timorous;
trepid; (∼ of aging) gerascophobic; (∼ of animals) zoophobic; (∼ of baldness) peladophobic; (∼ of bees) apiophobic; (∼
of cats) ailurophobic, aelurophobic, elurophobic, felinophobic,
gatophobic; (∼ of children) pedophobic; (∼ of choking) pnigophobic; (∼ of cold) psychrophobic; (∼ of colors) chromophobic;
(∼ of crowds) agoraphobic, demophobic, ochlophobic; (∼ of
darkness) nyctophobic, scotophobic; (∼ of daylight) phengophobic; (∼ of death) necrophobic,
thanatophobic; (∼ of deformity)
dysmorphophobic; (∼ of de-
mons) bogyphobic; (∼ of
deserts) xerophobic; (∼ of dining) deipnophobic; (∼ of dirt)
misophobic, musophobic, mysophobic; (∼ of disease) nosophobic, pathophobic; (∼ of disorder) ataxiophobic, ataxophobic;
(∼ of doctors) iatrophobic; (∼
of drafts) anemophobic; (∼ of
drinking) dipsophobic; (∼ of
drugs) pharmacophobic; (∼ of
dryness) xerophobic; (∼ of dust)
amathophobic; (∼ of eating)

phagophobic; (∼ of England)
Anglophobic; (∼ of error) hamartophobic; (∼ of everything)
panophobic; (∼ of examinations)
kopophobic; (∼ of excrement)
coprophobic, scatophobic; (∼ of
eyes) ommatophobic; (∼ of failure) kakorrhaphiophobic; (∼ of
fatigue) ponophobic; (∼ of fever) febriphobic, pyrexiophobic;
(∼ of filth) mysophobic, rhypophobic; (∼ of fire) pyrophobic;
(∼ of fish) ichthyophobic; (∼
of flowers) anthophobic; (∼ of
food) cibophobic; (∼ of foreigners) xenophobic; (∼ of France)
Francophobic, Gallophobic; (∼
of frogs) batrachophobic; (∼ of
funerals) taphophobic; (∼ of
gaiety) cherophobic; (∼ of
germs) bacillophobic; (∼ of
ghosts) spectrophobic; (∼ of
glass) crystallophobic, hyalophobic; (∼ of God) theophobic; (∼
of heart disease) cardiophobic;
(∼ of heat) thermophobic; (∼
of heights) aerophobic, batophobic, hypsiphobic, hypsophobic;
(∼ of home) ecophobic, oecophobic, oikophobic; (∼ of homosexuality) uranophobic; (∼ of
horses) hippophobic; (∼ of infection) molysomophobic; (∼ of
insanity) maniaphobic; (∼ of insects) entomophobic; (∼ of leprosy) lepraphobic; (∼ of lice)
pediculophobic; (∼ of light)
photophobic; (∼ of lightning)
astraphobic, keraunophobic, ceraunophobic; (∼ of liquids) hygrophobic; (∼ of lying) mythophobic; (∼ of marriage)

gamophobic; (~ of men) androphobic; (~ of mind) psychophobic; (~ of mirrors) catoptrophobic; (~ of missiles)
ballistophobic; (~ of mob) ochlophobic; (~ of monsters) dysmorphophobic, teratophobic; (~
of nakedness) nudophobic, nudiphobic; (~ of names) onomatophobic; (~ of needles) belonephobic; (~ of negligence)
paralipophobic; (~ of night)
noctiphobic, nyctophobic; (~ of
noise) acousticophobic, phonophobic; (~ of novelty) cainophobic; (~ of nudity) gymnophobic; (~ of odors)
osmophobic; (~ of pain) algophobic, odynophobic; (~ of
people) anthropophobic, demophobic; (~ of perversion) paraphobic; (~ of phantoms) spectrophobic; (~ of pins)
belonephobic; (~ of poisoning)
toxiphobic, toxicophobic; (~ of
pope) papaphobic; (~ of poverty) peniaphobic; (~ of preci-
pices) cremnophobic; (~ of
pseudorabies) kynophobic, cynophobic; (~ of rabies) hydrophobic; (~ of railroads) siderodromophobic; (~ of rain)
ombrophobic; (~ of red) erythrophobic; (~ of reptiles) herpetophobic, ophidiophobic; (~ of
responsibility) hypengyophobic;
(~ of rivers) potamophobic; (~
of sea) thalassophobic; (~ of
sex) coitophobic, cypridophobic,
erotophobic, genophobic; (~ of
sharks) galeophobic; (~ of sin)
hamartophobic; (~ of sinning)

peccatiphobic; peccatophobic; (~
of sleep) hypnophobic; (~ of
smells) olfactophobic; (~ of solitude) autophobic, eremiophobic,
eremophobic, monophobic; (~
of open spaces) agoraphobic, ce-
nophobic, kenophobic; (~ of
spiders) arachnephobic; (~ of
spirits) demonophobic; (~ of
stars) astrophobic, siderophobic;
(~ of stinking) bromhidrosipho-
bic, bromidrosiphobic; (~ of
sunlight) heliophobic; (~ of surgery) tomophobic; (~ of talking)
laliophobic, lalophobic; (~ of
tastes) geumophobic; (~ of
teeth) odontophobic; (~ of ter-
mites) eisoptrophobic, isopterophobic; (~ of thieves) kleptophobic, cleptophobic; (~ of
"13") tridecaphobic, triskaidekaphobic; (~ of thunder) brontophobic, keraunophobic, ceraunophobic, tonitrophobic,
tonitruphobic; (~ of toads) bac-
trachophobic; (~ of touching)
aphephobic, haphephobic, haptephobic; (~ of trembling) tremophobic; (~ of tuberculosis)
phthisiophobic; (~ of urinating)
urophobic; (~ of vomiting)
emetophobic; (~ of walking)
bathmophobic; (~ of war) traumatophobic; (~ of water) hydrophobic; (~ of weakness) as-
thenophobic; (~ of wealth)
chrematophobic; (~ of whirl-
pools) dinophobic; (~ of wine)
enophobic, oenophobic, oinophobic; (~ of women) gynephobic,
gynophobic; (~ of work) ergasiophobic, ergophobic; (~ of

worms) helminthophobic, scoleciphobic, vermiphobic.

feasibility, possible.

feather, mollipilose; (absence of ~s) nullipennate; (contour ~) pennaceous; pinnate, pinnated, pinnatifid; plumate, plumose; plumuliform.

feces, excremental; fecal, feculent; (fear of ~) coprophobic; (love of ~) coprophilic.

fee, emolumental.

feeding, edacious; threptic.

feeling, affectional, affectionate, affectionated; emotional; esthetic; passional, passionate; pathetic, pathetical; (lack of ~) stoic, stoical; (crawly ~) formicative.

feet, chiropodial; pedate; podiatric; podological; (feathered ~) ptilopaedic; (four ~) quadruped, quadrupedal; (large ~) sciapodous, skiapodous; (two ~) bipedal; (webbed ~) palamate; pediform, pedigerous.

feldspar, feldspathic; sanidinic.

felt, pannose.

female, distaff; effeminate; feminine; (~ form) gynecomorphous.

femur, crural.

fen, paludal, paludic, paludicolous.

fer-de-lance, bothropic.

fermentation, zymic, zymogenic, zymogenous; zymose, zymotic.

fern, filical, filiciform; pteridoid.

fertility, fecund; feracious.

fertilization, gamic; xenogamous.

fervency, ardent; warm-blooded.

festival, (~ of Ceres) Paganalian.

fever, aguish; calentural; febrific, febrile; pyretic; (~ cure) antipyretic; (fear of ~) febriphobic, pyrexiophobic.

fiber, flax; nemaline.

fibula, peroneal.

fiction, apocryphal; artificial; bogus.

fiddle, pandurate, panduriform.

field, agrestic; campestral.

fifty, quinquagesimal.

fig, ficoid; ficiform.

filament, capillaceous; catenulate; filiform.

filbert, corylaceous.

filling, expletive, expletory.

filth, feculent; lairy; nasty; ordurous; vile; (fear of ~) mysophobic; rhypophobic; (love of ~) mysophilic.

fin, (large ~s) macropterous.

finality, last; latemost; latest; ultimate; peremptory.

finance, fiscal.

finch, fringillid, fringilline, fringilliform.

finger, dactylous; digitate, digitiform; (absence of ~s) adactylous.

fingernail, onychoid; onychoidal; ungual; (divination using ~s) onychomantic.

fingerprint, dactylographic.

Finland, Suomic.

fire, igneous, igniform, ignigenous; phlogistic; (~ bug) pyromaniacal; (~ works) pyrotechnic, pyrotechnical; (~ worship) pyrolatric, pyrolatrous; (destruction by ~) incendiary, pyrogenic; (divination by ~) pyromantic, pyroscopic; (fear of ~) pyrophobic; (love of ~) pyrophilic.

firefly, lampyrid.
fireworks, pyrotechnic.
fir tree, abietineous.
fish, ichthyal, icthyic, icthyoid, icthyoidal; ichthyomorphic, icthyomorphous; piscine; pisciform; (~ eater) piscivorous; (divination using ~) ichthyomantic; (eating ~) ichthyophagian; ichthyophagous; (fear of ~) ichthyophobic; (worship of ~) ichthyolatrous.
fisherman, piscatory.
fishing, halieutic; piscatory, piscatorial; piscatological.
fissure, rhagadiform; rimate.
fit, adaptable, adaptative, adaptive.
fitness, idoneous.
five, pentaploid; pentamerous; quinary, quinquepartite.
flabbiness, myotonic.
flag, vexillary; vexillological.
flagellum, mastigophoric, mastigate, mastigote.
flake, laminable, laminar, laminary, laminate, laminated, laminose; scaly.
flame, alight.
flamingo, phoenicopteroid, phoenicopterous.
flash, bright; brilliant; lamping.
flashiness, jazzy.
flask, (~ shape) ampullaceous, ampullate, ampulliform; aryballoid; lageniform.
flatness, aclinal; horizontal; tabular; two-dimensional.
flattening, applanate; oblate.
flattery, gnathonic; sycophantic.
flatulence, carminative; ventose.
flatworm, planarian; platyhelminthic.

flavor, relished; sapid, saporous.
flaw, lacunal, lacunate, lacunary; naevoid; (absence of ~) perfect.
flea, pulicid, pulicine, pulicose, pulicous; (~ killer) pulicidal.
flesh, carnal, carneous, carnic, carniferous, carniform, carnose, carnous; creatic; sarcoline, sarcoid, sarcophilous, sarcotic, sarcous, sarcophagous; (~ eater) carnivorous, creophagous; (rare) omophagic; omophagous; (eating human ~) anthropophagous, cannibalistic.
fleur-de-lis, (heraldry) tressured.
flicker, lambent.
flight, aeronautical; aerotechnical; soarable; volant, volar, volitorial.
flightiness, anile; volage.
floating, buoyant; natant, supernatant.
flock, gregal, gregarian, gregarious.
flogging, (addicted to ~) verberative.
flood, diluvial; inundant; (~ gate) sluicy.
floor plan, ichnographic.
Florence, Florentine.
flounder, pleuronectid.
flour, farinaceous.
flourish, vernant.
flow, effluent; diffluent; fluxional; perfluent, profluent.
flower, anthophorous; floriated, florid, floriparous, florulent, floriform; (~ bearing) floriferous; (~ eater) anthophagous; (~ dweller) anthophilous; (cultivation of ~s) floricultural; (fear of ~s) anthophobic; (love of ~s) anthomaniacal; (regular ~s) isanthous.

flowering, efflorescent.
flowerpot, vasculiform.
fluid, (volcanic ∼) lava, lavatic, lavic; liquid.
fluorine, (*archaic*) phthoric.
fly, agromyzid; homopteran, homopterous; muscid, musciform; (fruit ∼) acalyptrate, drosophilid; (Mediterranean fruit ∼) trypetid; (scorpion ∼) mecopterous.
flycatcher, (∼ bird) muscicapine.
flying, aerodynamic; Icarian; volitant, volant; volitational, volitorial; (∼ in airplanes) aerodromic; (space-∼) astronautic.
foam, spumose, spumous, spumy.
fog, brumous; hazy; nubilous.
fold, flectional, flexional; plicatile.
folklore, storiological.
follicle, (*botany*) conceptacular.
food, alimental, alimentive; (*rare*) cibarian, cibarial, cibarious; dietetic, dietetical; nutrient, nutritional, nutritive; nurtural; pabulary, pabulous; papular; (enjoyment of ∼) epicurean; (fear of ∼) cibophobic; (undigested ∼) lienteric.
foolishness, desipient; fatuous; harish, insipient.
foot, (metrical ∼) anapestic, iambic, dactylic, trochaic.
foot, (bare ∼) discalced; (long ∼) dolichopodous; (spiny ∼) acanthopodus.
forbearance, longanimous.
force, emphatic; vehemency; violent.
forceps, forcipiform.
forearm, cubital.
forecast, prognosticative.

forehead, metopic; sincipital; frontal.
foreigner, alien; strange; tramontane; (fear or hatred of ∼s) xenophobic.
foreshadowing, adumbrative.
foresight, provident.
forest, Hylean; sylvan, silvan.
forestalling, obviable.
forewarning, precautional, precautionary, precautious.
forgery, counterfeit; fabricated; spurious.
forgetfulness, Lethean.
fork, bifurcate; divaricate; (*heraldry*) fourchée; furcate, furcellate.
form, idiomorphic, idiomorphous; morphologic; shaped; (description of ∼) morphographic; (unusual ∼) xenomorphic, xenomorphous; (land ∼) geomorphologic, geomorphological; (without ∼) adelomorphic, amorphic, amorphous, anidian, incorporeal.
formality, solemn.
formation, abstriction; poietic.
forsaking, lasslorn.
fortification, walled.
fortitude, longanamous.
fortune, lucky.
fortuneteller, haruspical, haruspicate.
forty, quadragesimal, quadragintesimal.
forward, antrorse.
forwardness, froward; impertinent; pert; saucy.
fossil, paleozoologic, paleozoological; (∼ animal) zoolithic, zoolitic; (∼ birds) paleornithologic, paleornithological; (∼ fish)

paleichthyological; (∼ footprints) ichnological.

founder, (*rare*) fundational.

fountain, fontal.

four, quadric, quadrifid, quadruple, quadruplex, quadruplicate, quaternary; tetradic; tetramerous.

fowl, (domestic) gallinaceous.

fox, alopecoid; vulpecular, vulpinic, vulpine; (∼ killing) vulpicidal.

fragility, breakable; brittle; frangible.

fragrance, ambrosial; aromatic; nosy; odoriferous; perfumy; redolent.

frailty, brittle; delicate.

France, Gallic, Gallican; (fear of ∼) Francophobic, Gallophobic; (love of ∼) Francophilic, Gallophilic.

frankincense, thuriferous.

fraud, covinous; fallacious, fallible; obreptitious.

freckle, lenticular, lenticulate, lentiform, lentigenous; macular.

freedom, disengaged; easy; (destruction of ∼) liberticidal.

freezing, cryogenic; (∼ point) cryoscopic.

frenzy, fanatic, fanatical; frantic; furibund, furied, furious; lymphatical; phrenetic; pythian.

friction, abradant, abrasive; (treating of disease by ∼) iatroliptic.

friend, amiable, amicable, amical; (killing of ∼) amicidal.

friendliness, amiable; hospitable.

frigate bird, pelecaniform.

fright, afraid; fearful; horrendous.

fringe, fimbrial, fimbriate; laciniate, laciniated, laciniform, lacini-
ose, lacinious, lacinulate, lacinulose.

frivolity, nidgety; shallow.

frog, batrachian; ranarian, ranine; (fear of ∼s) bactracophobic.

front, façadal, facial.

frost, frigorific; (*archaic*) frore; pruinate, pruinose, pruinous.

froth, barmy; spumose, spumous, spumy.

fructification, parturient.

fruit, carpological; feracious; (*heraldry*) fructed; fructiform; pomological; samariform; (∼ eater) carpophagous, fructivorous, frugivorous; (∼ producer) carpogenous, carpogenic; (rough ∼) trachycarpous.

fruit bat, megachiropteran, megachiropterous.

frying, sauté.

fugitive, (*rare*) profugate.

fulfillment, effectful, effectible, effective, effectual; satisfactional, satisfactive.

fullness, replete.

fun, apolaustic.

fundamentality, basal.

funeral, funebrial, funebrious; obsequial.

fungus, agaric, agariciform, agaricoid; fungoid; mycetous, mycoid, mycologic; (∼ eater) mycetophagous, fungivorous.

funnel, infundibulate, infundibuliform.

furnace, fornacic.

furniture, mobiliary.

furrow, guttery; vallecular, valleculate; sulcular, sulculate, sulciform, sulcate, sulcal.

fury, boisterous; furibund; madding; renish.

fusion, chiasmal, chiasmatic; karyogamic; syncretistic.

futility, defeatist; nugatory; otiose.

future, apocalyptic; necromantic; prophetic.

G

Gaelic, Goidelic.

gaiety, Anacreontic; galliard, galloptious; jolly; rorty.

gain, acquired, acquisite; lucrative; remuneratory; quaestuary.

galaxy, galactic; nebular, nebulescent.

gall, (∼ producer) cecidogenous.

gallantry, brave.

gallfly, cynipid, cynipidous, cynipoid.

gallows, (*archaic*) patibulate.

gallstone, cholelithic.

galvanometer, rheometric.

Ganges, cisgangetic.

gangrene, sphacelated.

gannet, pelecaniform.

gap, discontinuous; lacunal, lacunary, lacunulose.

gape, dehiscent; hiant; rictal.

gar, ganoid.

garishness, criant.

garlic, liliaceous.

garment, sartorial; vested, vestiary, vestmented.

gas, vaporable, vapored, vaporescence, vaporiferous, vaporing, vaporish, vapory.

gate, valval, valvate, valviferous, valvular.

gathering, conventicular.

gaudiness, brankie; criant.

gavial, eusuchian; loricate.

gelatin, tremelloid.

gem, lapidarian, lapidary, lapideous, lapidific, lapidose; lapilliform.

generic name, hyponymic, hyponymous.

generosity, liberal; magnanime, magnaminous; munific, munificent; warmhearted.

generousness, plenteous, plentiful, plenty.

geniality, bonhomous.

genitals, pudic, pudendal; venereal.

genius, daemonic.

genteelness, polite, politeful.

gentleness, mild; polite, politeful.

genuine, veridical, veridicous; veracious.

geography, (∼ of mountains) orographic, orographical; (∼ of wetlands) telmatological; (physical ∼) topologic, topological.

geology, (mineral ~) lithologic, lithological; (structural ~) geotectonic.

Georgia, (Soviet ~) Iberian; Kartvelian.

geranium, geraniaceous; rutaceous.

Germany, Gothonic, Gothic; Teutonic; (fear of ~) Teutophobic, Teutonophobic.

gesture, kinesic; cheironomic, chironomic.

ghost, spectral, spectrological; spooky; (belief in ~s) eidolistic; (divination using ~s) sciomantic; (fear of ~s) spectrophobic.

giant, Cyclopean, Cyclopic; rounceval; Titanesque; gigantic; huge; pachydermatous; behemoth.

gibbon, pongid; simiid.

giddiness, volage.

gill, branchial; (below the ~) infrabranchial; (~ cover) opercular, operculate; (~ parasite) branchicolous; (~ and heart) branchiocardiac.

gimbals, Cardanic.

ginger, zingiberaceous.

ginseng, araliceous.

giraffe, artiodactylous.

girdle, cingulate.

girl, (marriageable ~) nubile.

gland, acinotubular; adeniform, adenoidal, adenological; adenoneural, adenose; macrodenous.

glans, balanic.

Glasgow, Glaswegian.

glass, hyaline, hyalescent, hyaloid; vitreal, vitreous, vitric; vitriform; vitroan; (fear of ~) crystallophobic, hyalophobic; (writing on ~) crystographic.

gleam, bright; brilliant; vernicose.

glide, lambent, (*rare*) aerodonetic.

glimmer, crepuscular.

glitter, bright; brilliant.

globe, coccoid, coccous; spherical, spheric; orbital; spheroid, spheroidal, spheroidic.

globule, stilliform.

gloom, Cimmerian; dour; eerie; funereal; melancholic; morbid; morose; saturnine; stygian; tenebrose, tenebrous.

gloss, nitid, nitidous; splendent.

glossary, nomenclatorial, nomenclatural.

glow, candent, incandescent; noctilucent; perfervid.

glowworm, lampyrid; elaterid.

glue, colletic; colloid, colloidal; agglutinant; conglutinate, conglutinative; glutinose, glutinous; viscid, viscous.

glutton, epicurean; gourmand.

gnat, dipterous.

gnawing, arrosive; naggish; rosorial.

gnome, sylphic.

goat, artiodactylous; capric, caprid, caprine, caprinic; hircic, hircine, hircinous.

goblet, scyphiform; urceiform.

goby, gobiiform, gobiid.

God, ambrosial; deific, deiform; devine, yahwistic; theologic, theological, theomorphic; (~ -centered) theocentric; (~ in nature) pantheistic; (divination using ~s) theomantic; (eating ~s) theophagous; (fear of ~) theophobic; (hatred of ~) misotheistic; (inspiration of ~) theopneustic; (loved by ~) theophilic; (love for ~) philotheistic, theophilic; (many ~s) polytheistic; (one ~) monotheistic; (origin of ~s) theogonic; (physical manifestation of ~) theophanic; (possession by ~) theoleptic.

godwit, scolopacine.

goiter, strumose, strumous.

gold, aureate, auriferous, aurific, aurous; doré; (~ and ivory) chryselephantine; (~ writing) chrysographic; (dislike of ~) aurophobic; (lover of ~) chrysophilic; (rule by ~) chrysocratic.

goldfinch, cardueline.

goldfish, cyprinid, cyprinoid.

goodness, agathologic, agathological, benefic, beneficial; boniform; mabuti.

goose, anserine.

gooseberry, grossular.

gopher, sciuromorphic.

gorilla, pongid; simiid.

goshawk, accipitrid, accipitral, accipitrine.

gourd, cucurbitaceous.

gourmand, epicurean, epicureal.

gourmet, epicurean.

gout, podagral, podagric, podagrous.

government, archological; gubernative, gubernatorial; politic, political; (~ by army) stratocratic; (~ by equality) isocratic, pantisocratic; (~ by fathers) patriarchal; (~ by God) thearchic, theocratic; (~ by hereditary sovereign) monarchical; (~ by landowners) timocratic, timocratical; (~ by mob) ochlocratic, ochlocratical; (~ by mothers) matriarchal; (~ by mutual action) hamacratic; (~ by priests) hagiarchal, theocratic; (~ by slaves) dulocratic; (~ by the few) oligarchic, oligarchical; (~ by the many) polyarchical; (~ by the people) democratic; (~ by the wealthy) plutocratic; (~ by the worst men) kakistcratic; (~ by women) gynarchic, gyneocratic; (church ~) ecclesial, ecclesiastic, ecclesiastical; (elimination of ~) anarchic, nihilistic, (*rare*) antarchistic; (self-~) autonomous.

governor, gubernatorial; viceregal, viceroyal.

grace, elegant; gracile.

graciousness, benignant.

grain, cereal, cerealian, cerealic; grumose; (~ eater) granivorous; (~ field) segetal.

grammar, (violation of ~) solecistic.

granule, chondritic; grumose.

granulosity, chondritic.

grape, aciniform; botryoidal; vinaceous, vineal, vinifera; viticultural.

graphite, plumbaginous.

grasp, discernible, discerning.

grass, agrostographic, agrostologic, agrostological; gramineous; (~ dweller) graminicolous; (~ eater) graminivorous; (~ green) chlorine.

grasshopper, acridid, acridian.

gratification, satient, satisfied; voluptuous.

grave, (love of ~s) taphophilic.

gravel, calculous.

gravity, (center of ∼) centrobaric, centrobarical; serious.

grayness, griseous; grizzly; lyard.

grazing, rasant.

grease, pinguinitescent, pinguified; unctious, unctuous.

grebe, colymbiform.

Greece, Achaean; Argive; Attic; Helladic, Hellenic; Ionian.

greed, avaricious; esurient; pleonectic; (∼ for money) mammonish.

greenness, chlorochrous; verdant, verdigrisy, verdured; verte; virent, virescent, viridescent, viridigenous, viridine; (grass green) chlorine.

greeting, salutational, salutatious, salutiferous.

grief, dolorous, dolorific, doloriferous; heart-rending; heart-sore; languorous; moanful; mournful; sad; wailful.

grimace, rictal.

grin, rictal.

grinding, molar, molary, molinary; tritural.

gristle, cartilaginous, cartilagineous.

grit, sabellan, sabulous; tophaceous.

groin, inguinal.

groove, canalicular, canaliculate, canaliferous; cannelured; fossulate; sulcate; valleculate, vallecular.

ground sloth, xenthral.

groundwork, substrative.

group, agminate.

grouse, gallinaceous, galliform; phasianid.

grove, nemoral; (∼ of Diana) Nemorensian; (∼ dweller) nemoricole, nemoricoline, nemoricolous.

growing, (∼ on or in ground) geogenous; (∼ underground) geophilous.

growth, accrescent, accretionary, accretive; acervate; acrogenous; anisodynamous; auxetic; caruncular, carunculous; crescive; (excessive ∼) hypertrophic; (subnormal ∼) hypotrophic; neoblastic; (stunted ∼) pauperitic; (distorted ∼) acromegalic.

guardian, Cerberean, Cerberic; custodial.

guest, inquiline, inquilinous.

guide, cynosural.

guillemot, charadriiform.

guilt, culpable; nocent.

guinea fowl, phasianid.

guinea pig, hystricomorph, hystricomorphic, hystricomorphous.

gulf, discontinuous; voraginous.

gull, charadriiform; larid, larine, laroid.

gum, guttiferous; resinaceous, resinic, resinoid, resinous.

gums, periodontal, periodontic; peridental; uletic.

gushing, effusive.

gut, enteric; gastroenteric, gastroenterological; visceral.

gymnasium, palaestral, palaestrian, palaestric.

gymnastics, acrobatic; calisthenic.

H

H, (∼-shape) zygal.

habit, accustomed; addicted; habitual; frequent; usual.

hagfish, cyclostome, cyclostomate, cyclostomatous.

hair, barbate, barbellate; capillary, capilliform, capillose; comate, comose, comous; crinal, crinate, crinated, crinitory, crinose; hirsute; mollipilose, mollitious; pileous, piliferous, piliform, piline; setuliform, setulose; trichoid; villiform, villoid, villous; (∼ less) glabrate, glabrous, pilgarlicky; (covered with long ∼) jubate; (dark ∼) melanocomous, melanotrichous; (disease of ∼) trichopathic; (eating ∼) trichophagous; (gray ∼) grizzled, grizzly; (production of ∼) trichogenous; (red ∼) Judas-colored; (straight ∼) lissotrichous; (wooly ∼) ulotrichous.

haircloth, (*obsolete*) cilicious.

half-century, sesquicentennial.

Halifax, (Nova Scotia *or* Yorkshire) Haligonian.

halo, nimbused.

hammer, malleiform.

hand, chiral, chirological; manal, manual; (beautifying of ∼s) chirocosmetic; (divination using ∼s) chiromantic; (left ∼) kitthoge, kithogue; (study of ∼s) chirognomic; (two ∼s) bimanal, bimanous, bimanual.

handwriting, calligraphic, calligraphical; cheirographic, chirographic, cheirographical, chirographical; graphologic, graphological; (divination using ∼) graptomantic; (imitation of ∼) isographic, isographical.

hangover, crapulent.

happiness, ataractic, ataraxic; beatific; eudaemonic, eudemonical; euphoric; joyful; merry; (fear of ∼) cherophobic.

harangue, (*obsolete*) concionatory; demegoric; declamatory.

harassment, importunate.

harbinger, foreboding.

hardness, adamantine, adamantive; granitic; indurate, indurative.

hare, leporid, leporiform, leporine.

harlot, (love of ∼) philopornistic.

harm, deleterious; disserviceable; noisome; noxious; pernicious; scatheful.

harmony, (*rare*) concentive; neomodal; euphonic.

harshness, abusive; dispiteous; severe.

haste, (lack of ∼) slothful, slow, sluggish.

hat, castorial.

hatred, malevolent; rancorous; (∼ of foreigners) xenophobic; (∼ of sermons) homilophobic; (∼ of wine) enophobic, oenophobic, oinophobic; (∼ of women) gynephobic, gynophobic.

haughtiness, supercilious.

hawk, accipitral, accipitrine.

hazard, minatory; (*archaic*) parlous.

haze, foggy; nebulous.

hazelnut, corylaceous.

head, capitate; cephalate, cephaloid, cephalous; cranial, craniologic, craniological; (absence of ∼) acephalic, acephalous, acranial, acrocranial; (divination using ∼s) cephalomantic; (large ∼) macrocephalic, macrocephalous; (lionlike ∼) leontocephalous; (long ∼) dolichocephalic, dolichocephalous; (measurement of ∼) cephalometric, cephalometrical; (medium ∼) mesaticephalic; (short ∼) brachycephalic, brachycephalous; (small ∼) microcephalic, microcephalous; (*heraldry*: turned ∼) gardant; (two ∼s) bicephalous, dicephalous; (weasellike ∼) vareheaded.

healing, Aesculapian; cicatrisive, cicatrizant; Paeonian; sanable, sanative, sanatory; vulnerary.

health, buxom; hearty; hygienic; nicely; salubrious, salutiferous, salutory; sanitary; (good ∼) eucrasic, eucratic; (poor ∼) dyscrasic, dyscratic, valetudinarian.

heap, acervuline, acervative; aggerose.

hearing, aural, auricular; (measurement of ∼) acoumetric.

heart, cardiac, cardiacal, cardial, cardiologic, cardiological, cardiopathic; cordate, cordiform; obcordate; ventricular; (∼ shape) cardiod; (fear of ∼ disease) cardiophobic.

heartbeat, chronotropic.

heat, adiabatic; calefacient, calescent; caloric, calorific, calorifacient; candent; caumatic; (*rare*) excandescence, excandescent; febrile; feverish; (∼ from putrefaction) fracedinous; (fear of ∼) thermophobic; (measurement of ∼) calorimetric, thermometric; (movement of ∼) thermokinematic.

heathen, infidel, infidelic; nullifidian; pagan, paganic, paganistic; Pyrrhonistic.

heavens, aethereal, ethereal; celestial, celestine; empyreal, empyrean; firmamental; sublime; uranic.

heed, attent, attentive, attentional.

heel, calcaneal, calcanean.

height, altitudinal; lofty; (fear of ∼s) acrophobic, batophobic, hypsiphobic, hypsophobic; (measurement of ∼s) altimetric.

heir, (joint ~) coparcenary.

helmet, cassideous; galeiform.

help, accommodating; assistant, assistful; succorable.

hemisphere, (eastern ~) geontogeous.

hemp, cannabic; noggen.

herd, gregal, gregarian, gregarious.

herdsman, bucolic; pastoral.

heredity, familial; genetic.

hermit crab, pagurian.

hero, Argonautic; brave; Periclean; transpontine.

heron, grallatorial.

herring, clupeoid.

hesitation, juberous; dubious.

hiatus, lacunal, lacunary.

hiding, latent, latescent; secret, secretive.

highness, upper; superior.

hill, colliculate, collinal; knolly; tumulose; monticulate, monticulous.

hinge, (*zoology*) cardinal.

hip, coxal; ischial, ischiatic.

hire, hackney.

hissing, sibilant, sibilatory, sibilous.

hoariness, canescent.

hoarseness, roupy.

holding, (*Scottish*) habit.

hole, discontinuous; lacunal, lacunary, lacunose; (~ dweller) latebricole.

holiday, ferial; festal, festive.

holiness, sacred, sacre, sacrosanct; saint; sanct, sanctified.

hollow, cannulate, capsular.

holly, ilicaceous, ilicic.

home, (fear of ~) ecophobic, oecophobic, oikophobic.

homosexuality, gay; homoerotic; (fear of ~) uranophobic; (female ~) lesbian, sapphic, tribadic; (male ~) uranistic, urningistic.

honeycomb, alveolar, alveolate; cribiform; criblé.

honor, laureate, laurel.

hood, capistrate; cucullate, cuculliform.

hoof, ungulate, ungulous; (cloven ~ed) bisulcate.

hook, falcate, falcated; hamate, hamated, hamiform, hamular, hamulate, hamulose, hamulous.

horn, ceratoid; chitinous, chitinoid, chitogenous; corneous, cornigerous, corniculate, cornific, corniform, cornuate, cornuted; keratinous, keratoid, keratogenous, keratogenic; (~less) acerous, polled; (hollow ~) cavicorn; (one ~) monocerous; (two ~s) bicornate, bicornuate, bicornuous.

horse, caballine; chevaline; equine; hippoid; (diseases of ~s) hippiatric, hippopathologic; (fear of ~s) hippophobic; (lover of ~s) hippophilic; (taming of ~s) hippodamous.

horseshoe, hippocrepiform.

horseshoe crab, limuloid.

hospitality, xenial.

hostility, (*obsolete*) contrarious, contrary; inimicitious.

hotel, caravanserial.

house, domal.

housefly, cyclorrhaphous; dipterous.

household, domestic.

howl, ululant.

huckleberry, vacciniaceous.

hugeness, behemoth; Brobdingnagian; Cyclopean; elephantine; enormous; gargantuan; gigantic, gigantean; hippopotamic; immense; jumbo; monstrous; mountainous; pachydermatous; titanic.

hull, nautiform; wineglass.

humiliation, ignominious.

hummingbird, trochiline, trochilidine.

humor, Attic; facetious; farcical; jocose, jocular; jovial; Pantagruelian; Rabelaisian; satiric; Shavian.

hunchback, gibbous; kyphotic; scoliotic.

hundredfold, centuple, centuplicate.

hundredth, centesimal.

hunger, appetent, appetitive; esurient; ravening, ravenous; voracious.

hunting, cynegetic; venatic, venatical, venational, venatorial.

hurtfulness, harmful; nocuous, noxious; pernicious.

husband, (killing of ∼) mariticidal.

hydrophobia, rabic, rabid, rabietic, rabific, rabiform, rabitic.

hymn, lyric, lyrical.

hypnosis, mesmeric, mesmerizing.

hypocrisy, cant, Pecksniffian.

I

ice, crystic.

icon, (opposition to ~s) aniconic.

idea, notional.

identicality, consubstantial; Homoousian; same.

idiocy, cretinoid, cretinous; mongolic; mongoloid.

idleness, fainéant.

idol, (without ~s) aniconic.

idolatry, fetishistic.

illegitimacy, bastard; spurious.

illiteracy, analphabetic.

illness, sick, sickish, sickly; diseased; pathological.

illumination, luciferous, lucific, luciform; luminal, luminant, luminiferous, luminous.

illustration, sample; example; pictorial.

image, eidolic; iconological.

imagination, fantastic, fantastical; fictional.

imitation, allocryptic; artificial; echoic, echolalic; epigonic; facsimile; fake; mimetic, mimical; onomatopoeial, onomatopoeian, onomatopoeic, onomatopoetic; parodic, parodical; (*archaic*) sequacious; (faulty ~) cacozealous.

immaturity, boyish; neanic.

immeasurableness, (*obsolete*) immensive; cosmic.

immigrant, adventive.

immobility, cataplectic, cataleptic.

immoderation, disordinate; excessive.

immodesty, rampish.

immorality, evil; licentious; lascivious; obliquitous; prurient; salacious.

immortality, amaranthine; (*archaic*) eterne; perdurable; sempiternal.

immovability, adamant, adamantine.

impassivity, stolid.

imperialism, Kiplingese.

impetuosity, brash.

impiety, nefandous.

implication, questioning.

importance, kingly; momentous; serious; solemn; vital; essential.

impregnation, saturant; fertile.

improvement, eugenic; meliorist, melioristic.

impudence, brazen; Falstaffian; malapert; pert.

impulse, neuromotor.

inactivity, fainéant; laissez-faire.

incense, libaniferous, libanophorous, libanotophorous.

incident, episodic; eventful.

incivility, discourteous; rude; impolite.

inclination, acclivitous; dispositive; sloped.

incoherency, (speech ∼) disjointed; disorganized; jumbled.

incomprehensibility, acataleptic.

incongruity, grotesque.

incontiguousness, disjunct, disjunctional.

incorporation, absorbable, absorbefacient, absorptive; assimilable.

incorporeality, discarnate.

increase, crescent, crescive.

indecency, smutty; lewd.

indecision, vacillant, vacillatory.

indentation, crenelate, crenellate, crenelated, crenellated; crenelé; crenulate, crenulated.

independence, autonomous.

indifference, disdainful; insouciant; Laodicean; adiaphorous, adiaphoral.

indigenousness, endemic; autochthonous; native.

indigestion, dyspeptic.

individuality, laissez-faire; special.

indulgence, fond.

inebriation, Bacchanalian; besotted; jingled; squiffed; vinolent.

inexperience, kitling.

infant, babyish; neonatal; (killing of ∼) prolicidal.

infection, septic; viruliferous; (fear of ∼) molysomophobic.

infelicity, disconsolate; discontent; unhappy; unfortunate; unsuitable.

infidelity, adulterous; philandering; unfaithful, faithless.

infirmity, lame, lamish; senile; gimpy.

inflammation, exulcerate, ulcerative, ulcerous.

influence, affectable; momentous; operative, operatory; persuasive.

informality, shirt-sleeve.

information, advertisable; knowing.

informer, treacherous.

infrequency, occasional.

ingenuity, creative; Daedalian, Daedalic; original; skillful.

ingenuousness, artificial; contrived.

inhabitation, populous.

inharmony, disconformable, disconsonant.

inheritance, descendible; matrilineal, matrilinear; patrilineal, patrilinear.

inhumanity, dispiteous; cruel; uncaring.

injury, disserviceable; evil; harmful; noxious; pernicious; tortious; vulnerable.

injustice, iniquitous.

inn, caravanserial.

innocence, simple; exculpable; inculpable.

inoculation, vaccinatory.

inordinance, excessive.

inquiry, disquisitive; questionable.

insanity, (*archaic*) demonian; phrenetic; pythian; vesanic; (fear of ∼) maniaphobic.

inscription, epigrammatic, epigraphic.

insect, entomological; (fear of ∼s) entomophobic.

insensitivity, blunt, bluntish, blunted.

insincerity, disingenuous.

insipidness, foolish; namby-pamby; wishy-washy.

insolence, arrogant, arrogative; brazen; brassy.

insolvency, bankrupt.

inspiration, afflated.

instability, shaky.

instep, acrotarsial.

instruction, didactic, didactical; educated, educative; pedantic.

instrument, pentachordal; (stringed ∼) fidicinal; (wind ∼) aerophonic.

insubordination, disobedience; disorderly.

integrity, (lack of ∼) dishonest.

intellect, noetic.

intelligence, educated; knowing; sage.

intelligibility, articulate, articulative.

intemperance, crapulent; disordinate.

interbreeding, homogamic, homogamous.

intercourse, (sexual ∼) venereal.

interest, absorbing; agog.

interpretation, hermeneutic, hermeneutical.

interruption, caesural.

intersection, chiasmic, chiastic.

intestine, visceral.

intimacy, contubernal; familiar.

intolerance, totalitarian.

intoxication, alcoholic; Bacchanalian; squiffed; inebriate.

intrepidity, bold; valorous; fearless; brave.

intrigue, jesuitic; scheming, schemy.

inundation, clysmian.

inurbanity, discourteous.

invalid, valetudinaire, valetudinarian, valetudinary.

invalidity, nought; nugatory.

invention, fabricative.

investigation, disquisitive.

invigoration, bracing.

irascibility, choleric; warm-blooded; waspish, waspy.

Ireland, Hibernian, Hibernic.

iron, ferric, ferrous; Vulcanian, Vulcanic.

Iron Age, Villanovan.

irony, satiric, satirical.

irregularity, baroque.

irritability, erethic; fretful; peevish; techy, testy, touchy.

irritation, acerbate; bristly; exasperated; kickish.

Islam, Mohammedan; Moslem, Moslemic, Muslem, Muslim.

island, archipelagian, archipelagic; insular.

isolation, alone; secluded, seclusive; sole, solitary.

issuance, (*heraldry*) naissant.

Italy, Italic.

itch, pruriginous; urticant.

ivory, eburnated, eburnean, eburneoid, eburneous.

J

jacket, tabarded.
James I, Jacobean.
jaundice, icteric, icterical.
jaw, gnathal, gnathic; mandibular, mandibulary; maxillar, maxillary; (absence of ∼s) agnathous; (between ∼s) intermandibular. See also *projection*.
jelly, gelatinoid, gelatinous; glutinous; viscid.
jellyfish, discophorous; discophoran.
jeremiad, lamentatory.
jerk, saccadic.
Jesuit, Ignatian.
Jesus Christ, dominical.
Jews, Judaic, Judaical; Judaean, Judean.

John, Johannine.
joining, (*heraldry*) accollé.
joint, articular, articulary, articulate, articulated.
joke, jocose, jocular.
joker, facetious; waggish.
joy, enraptured, rapturous; blithe, blithesome; ecstatic; gladsome; happy.
judgment, discretional, discretionary.
jug, urceiform, urceolar, urceolate.
Jupiter, Jovial, Jovian; zenographic, zenographical.
Jura, (∼ mountains) cisjurane.
justice, (strict ∼) rhadamanthine.
justification, vindicable.

K

kangaroo, macropodine; (killing of
~) macropicidal.
keel, carinal, carinate, carinated,
cariniform; (two ~s) bicarinate.
kidney, nephric; renal.
killing, (~ of brother) fratricidal;
(~ of child) filicidal; (~ of father) patricidal; (~ of fox) vulpicidal; (~ of friend) amicidal;
(~ of husband) mariticidal; (~
of infant) prolicidal; (~ of kangaroo) macropicidal; (~ of king)
regicidal; (~ of mother) matricidal; (~ of old men) senicide;
(~ of oneself) suicidal; (~ of
parent) parricidal; (~ of
prophet) vaticidal; (~ of sister)
sororicidal; (~ of wife) uxoricidal; (~ of women) femicidal;
(mercy ~) euthanasic.
kindness, benignant; warmhearted.
king, (between ~s) interregal, in-
terregnal.
kiss, osculate, osculant, oscular, osculatory.

kitchen, cuisinary; culinary; scullery.
klipspringer, oreotragine.
knee, genuflexuous; geniculate, ge-
niculated.
knife, cultrate, cultrated; scalpelic.
knob, capitellate, capituliform;
nodulose; condyloid.
knot, carunculated; knarred,
knarry; nodated, noded, nodose,
nodous; nodiform.
knowledge, epistemic, epistemonic,
epistemologic, epistemological;
erudite; gnostic, gnostical; pun-
ditic; sapient, sapiential; (~
through questions) maieutic; (hatred of ~) misologistic; (love of
~) epistemophiliac; (superficial
~) sciolistic, sciolous; (universal
~) pansophic, pansophistical,
pantologic, pantological, polyhis-
toric, omniscient; (useful ~)
chresotomathic.
knuckle, condylar, condyloid.

L

labor, (*archaic*) elaborate; operose; Sisyphean, Sisyphian.

lac, resinaceous, resinic, resinoid, resinous.

laceration, discoid.

ladder, scalar, scalariform.

lake, lagoonal; lochy; (~ dweller) lacustrian, lacustrine, lacustral; (glacier ~) glaciolacustrine.

lambskin, budge.

lameness, claudicant; halting.

lamentation, threnetic; wailful, wailsome.

lamp, lucernal, lucigen.

lampoon, pasquilant, pasquilic.

lamprey, cyclostome, cyclostomate, cyclostomatous.

lancelet, cephalochordal, cephalochordate.

land, cadastral; praedial, predial; (~ and water) amphibious, amphibiotic.

landholding, feudal, feudalistic, feudatorial.

language, coprolaliac; linguistic, linguistical; (ambiguity of ~) amphibological, amphibolous, (artificial ~) pasigraphic; (bombastic ~) fustian, grandiloquent, lexiphanic, turgid; (clear ~) lucid, luculent, pellucid; (correct ~) orthological; (courtly ~) aulic; (dull ~) pedestrian; (illiterate ~) vulgarian; (having many ~s) multilingual, polyglot; (having one ~) monolingual; (having two ~s) bilingual; (informal ~) colloquial; (longwinded ~) aedistic; (nonsensical ~) jabberwockian; (obscure ~) Gongoristic, Gongoresque, periphrastic; (of two ~s) macaronic; (patterns of ~) morphological; (popular ~) demotic; (redundant ~) pleonastic.

languishing, lackadaisical.

lap, gremial.

lapse, caducous; labile.

lard, butyraceous; oleaginous.

lasting, aeonic; perennial; eternal.

latency, delitescent; dormant, dormient.

lateness, (~ in developing) serotinal, serotine, serotinous.

latex, laticiferous.

lattice, cancellate; clathrate, clathrulate.

laughter, cachinnatory; risible; (excessive ~) Abderian.

lava, vesiculous.

law, legal, legific; litigious; nomological, nomothetic; (drafting ~) nomographic, nomographical; (harsh ~) Draconian.

lawsuit, actionable.

laxative, chalastic; lapactic; cathartic; purgative.

layer, laminable, laminar, laminary, laminate, laminated, laminose; stratiform; (two ~s) bistratal.

laziness, sloth.

lead, galenoid; plumbean, plumbeous, plumbous, plumbic.

leader, demagogic; principal; shogunal; (chorus ~) choragic.

leadership, hegemonic, hegemonical.

leaf, allagophylous; foliaceous, foliicolous; foliiform; (fleshy ~) chylophyllous; (loss of leaves) deciduous; defoliate; phylloid; (two leaves) bifoliate, diphyllous; (three leaves) trefoil, trifoliate, trifoliated.

leafhopper, jassid.

leak, nailsick.

leaning, propense.

leanness, macilent.

leaping, (*heraldry*) salient; saltatorial.

learnedness, polymath, polymathic.

learner, discipular.

learning, chrestomathic; (*obsolete*) lered; paidentic, paedentic; pedantic; pedagogic, pedagogical.

leather, coriaceous.

leavening, (absence of ~) azymous.

leavetaking, apopemtic; valedictory.

leech, hirudinoid.

leek, prasine.

legacy, legatorial.

legend, fabled, fabulous.

leggings, ocreated, ocrecite.

legislation, (*obsolete*) disciplinary; nomological.

legitimacy, legal.

legs, shamble; (short ~) breviped.

leisure, otiose; vacational.

lending, usurious, usurous.

length, disemic; (lack of ~) short.

Lent, quadragesimal.

leper, lazarly, lazarous.

leprosy, (fear of ~) lepraphobic.

lesion, discoid.

lethargy, hebetudinous; (medicine) cataphoric.

letter, (alphabet) literal; (one ~) uniliteral.

level, complanate; even.

lever, homodromous.

lewdness, harlot; ithyphallic; laches; lecherous.

Leyden Jar, Kleistian.

liability, justiciable.

liberality, bounteous, bountied, bountiful.

liberation, extricable.

liberty, free.

lice, pedicular; (destructive to ~) pediculicide; (fear of ~) pediculophobic.

licentiousness, pornerastic.

lichen, epiphloedal, epiphloedic; usneoid; verrucatiaceous.

lick, lambitive.

life, macrobian, macrobiotic; vital; vivacious; zoetic.

ligament, alivincular; desmoid; (two ∼s) amphidesmous.

light, luciferous, lucific, luciform; luminal, luminant, luminiferous, luminous; pellucid; photic; photological; (fear of day ∼) phengophobic; (fear of ∼) photophobic; (impenetrable by ∼) opaque; (reflecting ∼) catoptric, catoptrical; (refracting ∼) dioptric; (transmitting ∼) translucent.

lightening, levigable.

lightning, (fear of ∼) astraphobic, ceraunophobic, keraunophobic; (thunder and ∼) fulmineous, fulminous.

likelihood, probable.

likeness, iconic.

lily, crinoid, crinoidal.

lime, (mineral) calcareous.

limit, circumscript.

limp, claudicant; halt.

lineage, pedigraic.

linen, (∼ from Colchis) sardonic.

lingering, slow; slug, sluggish.

link, concatenate; gimmal.

lintel, (*obsolete*) hanced.

lip, apilary; labeloid; labial, labiate, labiated; labral; labrose; (∼s and teeth) labiodental; (two ∼s) bilabial, bilabiate.

liquid, acetonic; fluent; fluid, fluidal; (dread of ∼) hygrophobic.

list, nomenclatorial, nomenclatural.

listening, audient, auscultatory.

literalness, Capernaitic.

liveliness, peppy.

liver, hepatic, hepatological; jecoral.

lizard, lacertiform, lacertilian, lacertiloid, lacertine, lacertoid.

load, laden.

loafer, larrikinism; slovenly.

loathsomeness, disgustful, disgusting.

lobe, ear-leaved; uvular; (two ∼s) bilobate, bilobated, bilobed, bifid; (three ∼s) trilobate, trilobated, trilobed, trifid; (four ∼s) quadrifid; (ten ∼s) decalobate.

localness, (absence of ∼) azonic.

location, situal; (abnormal ∼) ectopic; (normal ∼) entopic.

lock, sluicy.

logic, analytic; (*French*) raisonné.

London, cispontine.

loneliness, sole, solitary.

loop, fundiform.

loquacity, babblative, babblesome, babbling; gabby; linguacious.

loudness, boisterous; stentorian, stentorious.

lout, boorish.

love, Aphrodistic.

loveliness, beauteous, beautiful.

lowlands, Lallan.

lowness, evil; nadiral; nether, nethermost.

loyalty, allegiant; leal.

Loyola, Ignatian.

lozenge, (*heraldry*) mascled; urdy, urdé.

lucidity, sane.

luck, (lack of ∼) dismal.

luminescence, candescent.

lump, flocculable; nuggety.

lumpfish, cyclopteroid, cyclopterous.

lung, pulmonate, pulmonary, pulmonic; (between ∼s) interpulmonary.

lust, concupiscent; epithymetic, epithymetical; lecherous; rammish.

luster, (∼ of uncut precious stones) naif.

luxury, Corinthian; epicurean.

lying, Cyllenian; mendacious; (fear of ∼) mythophobic; (pathological ∼) pseudomaniacal; (propensity for ∼) mythomaniacal.

lyric, Anacreontic; madrigalian.

M

macaw, psittacine.
mackerel, acanthopterygian; scombrid, scombriform.
madness, fanatic, fanatical.
magic, Chaldean; necromantic; numinous; prestidigitatorial, prestidigitory; sortilegic, sortilegious; talismanic; thaumaturgic; theurgic; theurgical; Zendaic.
magician, mageiric; thaumaturgic.
magistrate, archontic; praetorial.
magnanimity, heroic.
magnesium, mafic.
magnification, macroscopic; megascopic.
magnificence, grand; majestic.
magpie, corvoid.
maiden, nymphal, nymphean, nymphical.
maieutics, hebamic.
making, factive.
malevolence, evil.
malformation, teratological.
malice, splenetic; acrimonious.
malignment, pernicious.
mammal, hematothermal; therologic, therological.
man, andric; hominal, hominine; (fear of men) androphobic; (killing of old men) senicide.
management, administerial, administrable, administrative; economic; kittle.
Manchester, Mancunian.
mandate, preceptive, preceptory.
mane, jubate.
manganese, manganic.
mange, scabietic.
mangling, lacerable, lacerant, lacerated, lacerative.
mania, cacoethic.
manic depression, cyclothymic.
mankind, (affection for ~) philanthropic; (hatred of ~) misanthropic.
manor, domanial; (rare) manerial; (lord of the ~) seignorial.
mansion, palatial, palatinal.
mantle, chlamydate.
manuscript, palimpsestic; (papyrus ~) papyrological.
map, cartographic, cartographical; chorographic; geographic; ichnographic; topographic.
marble, marmoreal; mirled.

margin, bordered; limbiferous.

mariner, sailor.

maritime, halimous; nautic, nautical.

market, nundinal.

marketing, circumforaneous.

marlin, istiophorid.

marmoset, callithricid.

marmot, sciurid, sciuromorphic.

marriage, affinal; conjugal, conjugial, jugal; connubial; hymneal; hypergamic, hypergamous; matrimonial; nuptial; (~ poem) epithalamic; (~ to one husband) monandrous; (~ to one partner) monogamous; (~ to several husbands) polyandric, polyandrous; (~ to several wives) polygynous; (~ to two partners) bigamous; (fear of ~) gamophobic; (hatred of ~) misogamic; (longing for ~) gamomanic; (second ~) deuterogamic, digamous.

marrow, medullary.

Mars, Arean; areologic, areological; areocentric.

marsh, (~ dweller) helobious; helodes; paludal, paludic, paludicolous; palustral, palustrian.

martin, hirundinous.

marvel, mirific.

masculinity, male.

mask, larvate.

masochism, algolagnic.

mass, agglomerate, agglomeratic, agglomerative; flocculable; nuggety.

massiveness, Cyclopean, Cyclopic.

master, kingly.

mastiff bat, molossid.

masturbation, onanistic.

matching, (absence of ~) odd.

materialism, Capernaitic.

mathematics, (love of ~) philomathic, philomathical, philomathean.

matrimony, conjugal, conjugial; connubial.

matter, hylic.

maturation, adult.

mausoleum, tombal.

maxim, aphoristic.

mayfly, plectopteran, plectopterous.

maze, circuitous; circumlocutory; daedal, Daedalian, Daedalic; labyrinthal, labyrinthian, labyrinthic, labyrinthiform, labyrinthine.

meadow, pratal; (~ dweller) pratincolous.

meadowlark, icterine.

meal, prandial.

mealworm, tenebrionid.

mealybug, hemipterous, hemipteroid.

meaning, semeiologic; semantic; (many ~s) polysemous.

meanness, caitiff; ignoble.

measles, morbillary, morbilliform, morbillous; rubeolar.

measurement, aerometric; mensural; metric, metrical; metrological; (~ of electricity) rheometric; (universal ~) pantometric, pantometrical.

meat, creatic; (~ eater) creophagous, carnivorous.

medal, numismatic.

medicine, Aesculapian; iatric; Paeonian.

meditation, ruminative.

meiosis, pachytene.

melancholy, atrabilar, atrabilarian, atrabilarious; dispirited; sad.

melody, ariose, arioso; canorous; cantabile; melopoeic, melopoetic; plagal.

melon, cucurbitaceous.

melting, deliquescent; syntectic.

membrane, hymenoid; lamellar, lamelliform; laminar; lammose; scarious.

memory, mnesic, mnestic; mnemonic; (lack of ∼) amnesic.

menace, minatory.

menhaden, clupeid.

menhir, dolmenic; monolithic.

menses, catamenial.

menstruation, emmenic; menorrheic.

merchandise, emporetic, emporeutic.

mercy, eleemosynary; humane; lenient, lenitive.

mess, sloppy, slovenly.

message, nunciative.

messenger, internuncial; internunciary.

metalworker, Cabirean, Cabirian, Cabiric, Cabiritic.

metaphor, allegoric, allegoristic; tralatitious.

meteorite, aerolitic, aerolithological.

meteorology, aerological.

midbrain, mesencephalic.

middle, mesal, mesial, mesothetic.

midwife, obstetric; tocological, tokological.

mildew, mucedinous.

military, (Japanese ∼) Shogunal.

milk, colostral, colostric, colostrous; galactoid, galactophorous; lactary, lacteal, lactean, lacteous, lactescent, lactic, lactiferous, lactific, lactifluous; lactiform.

milkweed, asclepiadaceous.

Milky Way, galactic.

mill, molinary.

millenarian, chiliastic.

millennium, chiliadic, chiliadal.

millepede, arthropodal, arthropodan.

mimicry, mimetic; synaposematic.

mind, gnostic; noetic; nooscopic; phrenic; psychic, psychical, psychogenic; (development of ∼) psychogonical; (fear of ∼) psychophobic.

mine, cunicular.

mineral, siliceous.

mink, mustelid.

minnow, (freshwater ∼) cyprinid, cyprinoid.

miracle, theurgic; thaumatological, thaumaturgic.

mire, guttery; lairy.

mirror, reflected, reflectant, reflective; reflexed; refringent; (fear of ∼s) catoptrophobic.

mirth, jocund.

mischief, harmful; naughty.

misplacement, disoriented.

missile, ballistic; (fear of ∼s) ballistophobic.

mist, brumous; foggy; hazy; nebulous; nubilous.

mistake, erroneous.

mite, acarian, acaridan, acariform, acaroid; demodectic; tarsonemid; (∼ killer) acaricidal; miticidal.

mitigation, alleviated, alleviative; assuasive.

mix, farraginous.

mixture, (∼ in a gland) heterocrine.

moa, ratite.

mob, gregal, gregarian, gregarious; (∼ rule) ochlocratic, ochlocratical; (fear of ∼) ochlophobic.

mockery, burlesque; derisive, derisory.

mockingbird, mimine; turdine.

model, archetypal, archetypical; normal, normative; paradigmatic.

moderation, temperant.

modernity, neoteric; new.

modesty, pudibund; shamefaced, shamefast, shameful; shy; verecund.

modification, aggradational.

modifier, (noun ∼) adnominal; (verb ∼) adverbal, adverbial.

moisture, aquose; humid, humific; juicy; madid.

molasses, treacly.

mold, mucedinaceous, mucedinous.

molding, alloplastic; architraved.

mole, talpoid, talpid; (marsupial ∼) notoryctid.

mole rat, spalacid.

mollification, mild.

mollusk, malacological; veligerous; (∼ eater) molluscivorous; (∼ shape) donaciform.

molting, exuvial.

monastery, cenobian.

money, numismatic; nummary, nummular; (∼ changing) nummulary; pecuniary; (lack of ∼) penurious.

mongoose, herpestine; viverrid, viverriform, viverrine.

monitor lizard, varanid.

monk, anchoretic, anchoritic; ce-

nobian, cenobitic; monachist, monochal; monastic.

monkey, pithecoid; simian.

monolith, dolmenic.

monopolization, engrossed.

monotony, samesome.

monotreme, implacental, implacentate.

monster, teratoid; teratological; Typhonian; (fear of ∼) dysmorphophobic, teratophobic; (love of ∼s) teratostic.

month, draconic; mensual, mensural, mensurative.

monument, cenotaphic.

moon, lunar; selenological; (divination using ∼) seleuomantic; (full ∼) plenilunal; (mapping of ∼) selenographic, selenographical; (new ∼) novilunar; (waning ∼) decrescent; (worship of ∼) selenolatrous.

moor hen, gallinuline; ralliform, ralline.

moose, cervid, cervine.

morality, deontological; (*archaic*) didascalic; ethical.

moray eel, muraenoid.

morning, matinal, matutinal.

morning glory, convolvulaceous.

mortal, human.

mortality, lethal.

mosaic, tessellar.

Moscow, Muscovite.

Moses, Mosaic.

mosquito, aedine; culicid, culicine; dipterous; nematoceran, nematocerous; (malarial ∼) anopheline.

moss, muscose, muscoid; (∼ dweller) muscicolous; (reindeer ∼) cladoniaceous, cladonioid.

moth, arctian; lepidopteral, lepidopterous; (clothes ~) tineid; (tiger ~) arctiid.

mother, maternal; matriarchic, matriarchal, matriarchical; matripotestal; (derived from ~'s name) metronymic; (killing of ~) matricidal.

mother-of-pearl, nacre; nacred; nacreous.

motion, (air ~) katabatic; (backward ~) palinal; (body ~) gestical, gesticular, gesticulacious, gesticulant, gesticularious, gesticulative, gesticulatory; kinematic; kinesic, kinetic, kinetical, kinetogenic; (circular ~) stobic; (lack of ~) stagnant; (sensation of ~) kinesthetic.

mound, tumular, tumulose.

mountain, alpine, cisalpine; cismontane, citramontane; orogenetic, orogenic, orological; montane, tramontane; (measurement of ~s) orometric; (love of ~s) acrophilic.

mournfulness, lachrymose.

mourning, lamentable, lamentational, lamentatory, lamented, lamentive; luctiferous, luctual; lugubrious, lugubrous.

mouse, (marsupial ~) dasyurid; myomorph, myomorphic; murid, muriform, murine; musine.

moustache, mystacial, mystacine.

mouth, actinostomal; buccal; intraoral; stomatal, stomatic, stomatous; stomatologic, stomatological; (~ and face) orofacial; oscular; (by ~) nuncupative, nuncupatory; (large ~) macrostomatous; (roof of ~) palatal, palated, palatine; (small ~) microstomatous.

mouthpart, (insect ~s) cibarian.

movability, portable, portatile, portative.

movement, active; agile, agitated; peripatetic.

moving, ambulant, ambulatory.

Mt. Ida, Idean.

mucus, blennoid; myxoid.

mud, guttery; limous; sallow; sapropelic; (~ dweller) limicolous; (~ swallower) limivorous.

muddle, stupefacient, stupefied.

mullet, mugiloid.

multitude, (*archaic*) gregal; plethoric.

mumps, parotitic.

munificence, liberal; lavish.

murk, fuliginous; tenebrose, tenebrous.

murmur, fremescent.

murre, charadriiform.

muscle, myogenic; myologic, myological; sarcous; (~ pain) myalgic.

muscularity, athletic.

Muses, Castalian.

mushroom, agaricic, agaricoid, agariform; (~ eater) mycophagous.

music, harmonic, harmonious, harmonical; Euterpean; lyric, lyrical; notational; (funeral ~) threnodic; (love of ~) philharmonic.

musician, Asaphic.

musk, moschiferous.

muskellunge, esociform.

muskrat, cricetid.

musk ox, bovine.

muslin, tarlatanned.
mussel shell, mytiliform.
mutilation, maimed.
mutism, alalic.
myrtle, lythraceous.
mystery, arcane; cabalic, cabalistic,

cabalistical; sibyllic, sibylline; telestic; tenebrous.
mystic, anagogic; orphic.
mysticism, mystagogic, mystagogical.
myth, apocryphal; fabled, fabulous.

N

nail, (*heraldry*) cloué; (∼ of the finger or toe) ungual, unguiculate, ungular.

naivety, simple.

nakedness, adamitic; nude; (fear of ∼) nudiphobic, nudophobic.

name, appellative; eponymic, eponymous; hyponymic, hyponymous; metonymic, metonymical; nomenclatural, nomenclatorial, nomenclative; nominative; onomasiologic, onomasiological; onomastic; (bad ∼) caconymic; (derived from one's child's ∼) paedonymic; (derived from father's ∼) patronymic; (derived from mother's ∼) matronymic, metronymic; (divination using ∼s) onomantic; (fear of ∼s) onomatophobic; (pet ∼) hypocoristic; (place ∼) toponymic, toponymical; (preoccupation with ∼s) onomatomaniacal.

nape, nuchal.

Naples, Neapolitan.

narcissism, autophilic.

narrowing, coarctate.

narrowmindedness, parochial; philistine; (*rare*) gigmanistic.

narrowness, dolichoid.

nasal cavity, ethmoid; mycteric.

nasturtium, tropaeolaceous.

nation, gentilic; (one's own ∼) domestic.

nationalism, chauvinistic; jingoistic.

native, aboriginal; autocthonous; indigenous; primary, prime; vernacular.

nativity, genuine.

natural frontier, arcifinious.

natural law, nomic.

nature, physiosophic, physiosophical; physiurgic; thaumatographic; (different ∼) allogeneous; (worship of ∼) physiolatrous.

nausea, qualmish; queasy.

nautilus, argonautid.

navel, omphalic; umbilical, umbilicate.

navigation, (aerial ∼) aeromarine; (naval ∼) maritime, marine; nautic, nautical.

nearness, nigh; proximal, approximal, approximate, approximative; contiguous; (*rare*) propinquitous, propinquous.

nearsightedness, myopic.

neatness, compt; natty.

nebula, turbid; cloudy; nepheloid.

necessity, essential; needful; obligatory.

neck, cervical; colliform; jugular; napal; nuchal; trachelate.

necklace, moniliform, monilioid, monilated.

necromancy, (*archaic*) goetic, goetical.

nectar, (~ eater) mellisugent, mellivorous.

need, necessitous.

needle, acicular, aciculate; belonoid; (fear of ~) belonephobic.

needlefish, belonid.

neglect, disregardful; forgetful; laches; lapsed, lapsing; omissible, omissive.

negligence, (fear of ~) paralipophobic.

neighbor, accolent; vicine, vicinal.

neighborhood, vicinal.

nematocyst, cnidarian, cnidophorous.

nephew, nepotal.

neophyte, catechumenal, catechumenical; novitial.

nerve, gangliac, ganglial, gangliar, gangliform, ganglioform, ganglioid, ganglionic, ganglionary; neural, neurological, neurosal; (~ sheath) epilemmal; (debility of ~s) neurasthenic; (description of ~s) neurographic, neurographical; (inflammation of ~s) neuritic; (pain in ~s) neuralgic; (sympathetic ~s) trisplanchnic.

nervousness, jittery; jumpy.

nest, caliological; (*rare*) nidamental; nidatory; nidological; (~ building) nidificant; (~ dweller) altricial, nidicolous.

nestling, nidulant, nidulate.

net, retiary, reticulate, retiform.

nettle, urticaceous, urtical, urticose.

network, plexiform; reticulate.

neutrality, adiaphorous, adiaphoral.

newborn, neonatal.

New England, Novanglian, Novanglican.

newt, tritonic.

niche, aedicular.

nickel, niccolous, niccolic.

night, nocturnal; (~ and day) nychthemeral; (~ blindness) nyctalopic; (fear of ~) noctiphobic, nyctophobic.

nightingale, (*obsolete*) philomelian.

nightmare, cacodemoniac, cacodaemoniac, cacodemonic, cacodaemonic; (*obsolete*) cacodemonial, cacodaemonial; mare-rode.

nimbleness, volant.

nine, nonuple; novenary, novene.

ninety, nonagesimal.

nipple, mammillar, mammillary, mammillate, mammilliform, mammilloid.

Noah, Noachian, Noachic, Noachical, Noaic.

nodding, nutant, nutational.

noise, cacophonic, cacophonous; fremescent; obstreperous; strepitous, strepitant; uproarious; vo-

ciferous; (fear of ∼) acousticophobic, phonophobic.

nomad, migrant, migrative, migra-
torial, migratory; Saracenic.

noncompliance, disconformable;
disconsonant; recusant.

nonreturn, irremeable.

nonsense, blithering.

noose, laquearian.

normality, ordinal, ordinary; regular; average.

north, boreal, borean; hyperboreal,
hyperborean.

Northman, Varangian.

North Pole, arctic.

nose, mycteric; narial; nasal, nasa-
logical; nasutiform; nostriled;
paranasal; proboscidal, proboscidate, proboscidial, proboscidiform, proboscidiferous; rhinal,
rhinogenous, rhinologic, rhinological; (large ∼) nasute; (narrow ∼) leptorrhinian.

nosebleed, rhinorrhagic.

nostril, narial, nariform; (paired
∼s) dirhinous; (single ∼)
monorhinal.

notch, (*heraldry*) raguly; indented;
crenelated.

nothing, nihilistic, nihilist.

nothingness, nihilitic.

notice, edictal.

notochord, chordal, chordate,
chordoid.

notoriety, famous, infamous.

nourishment, alimental, alimentary, alimentative, alimentic; nutritional, nutritionary, nutrimen-
tal, nutritive, nutritory,
nutritious; pabular, pabulary,
pabulous.

Nova Scotia, Acadian.

novelty, esoteric; (fear of ∼) cainophobic, cainotophobic; (hatred
of ∼) misoneistic; neophobic;
(love of ∼) neophilic; (worship
of ∼) neolatrous.

novice, novitial.

noxiousness, pernicious; insalubri-
ous; unwholesome.

nozzle, vermorel.

nucleus, karyologic, karyological,
karyotic.

nudibranch, aeolid.

nudity, adamitic; naturistic; (fear
of ∼) gymnophobic.

number, arithmetic, arithmetical;
digital; numerary, numerical, numerable, numeral, numerate,
numerative; (divination using
∼s) arithmomantic; (obsession
with ∼s) arithmomaniacal; (oc-
cultism using ∼s) numerological.

numbness, torpid, torpescent.

nun, monastic.

nuptial, bridal; (∼ song) epithalamic, epithalamial.

nursing, nutricial.

nut, nuciform.

nuthatch, sittine.

nutmeg, myristaceous.

nutrition, alimentological; trophic;
trophodynamic; trophogenic; trophoplasmatic, trophoplasmic;
trophotherapeutic; trophotropic;
(lacking ∼) jejune; (plant ∼)
agrobiologic.

nymph, (lake ∼) limniadic;
(mountain ∼) oreadic; (tree ∼)
hamadryadic; (wood ∼) dryadic.

O

oak, cupuliferous; quercine; (composed of ~ leaves) quernal.

oar, remiform.

oarfish, regalecid.

oath, juratory.

obedience, (*archaic*) buxom; duteous, dutiful; morigerous, morigerate.

obesity, liparoid, liparous, lipogenous; stout; fat; pinguid, pinguedinous, pinguescent, pinguitudinous.

obfuscation, obliquitous.

obituary, necrologic, necrological.

object, accusative.

objection, objurgatory; recusant.

obligation, deontic; jural.

obliqueness, bevel, beveled; aslant.

obliteration, effaceable.

obscenity, coprological; Fescennine; ithyphallic; nasty; scatologic, scatological; smutty; (love of ~) coprophilic.

obscurity, caliginous; hazy; larvate; nameless; arcane; recondite; tenebrose, tenebrous.

obsequiousness, sycophantic; toadying.

obsolescence, archaic, archaical, archaistic.

obstetrics, hebamic; maieutic.

obstinacy, bullheaded; pigheaded; stubborn.

obstruction, occludent.

obtuseness, blunt, bluntish; stupid.

Occident, Hesperic, Hesperian; western.

occult, arcane; Chaldean; cryptic.

occupation, absorbed; busy; engrossed; professional; versed.

ocean, bathal, bathypelagic; cisoceanic; marine; maritime; thalassic.

odor, aromatic; nidorous; olfactological, olfactory; osphretic; osmological, osmonological; (dependency on ~s) osmic; (fear of ~s) olfactophobic, osmophobic; (hatred of ~s) osphresiophobic; (love of ~s) osphresiophilic; (perception of ~s) osmatic.

offense, affrontive; aggressive; obscene; scandalous; scarlet.

offensiveness, disgustful, disgusting.

offering, sacrificable, sacrificatory; sacrificial.

oil, oleose, oleous, oleaginous, oleiferous; unctious, unctuous.

oilbird, caprimulgid, caprimulgiform.

okapi, giraffid, giraffoid.

Old World, gerontogeous.

omen, ominous; (*obsolete*) prodigious; augurous, augural; premonitory; prognostic; predictive; portentous.

omission, disregardful; neglectful, neglective.

omnipotence, almighty.

omnipresence, (*rare*) ubiquious; ubiquitarian, ubiquitous.

one, monoeidic; single, singular; unitary, unific, unary.

oneness, single, singular; unity.

one year, (∼ old) annotinous.

onion, cepaceous; liliaceous; (smell of ∼) alliaceous.

onomatopoeia, imsonic.

onyx, onychin.

opalescence, cymophanous.

open-air, al fresco; plein-air.

opening, discontinuous; orificial; ostiolar.

opium, opiatic, opiate; papaveraceous, papaverous.

opossum, didelphine, didelphid.

opprobrium, flagitious; nefarious; (*obsolete*) scelerous.

optimism, sanguine; upbeat.

oracle, vatic; prophetic; sybilline, sybilic, sybillic; orphic.

oralness, nuncupative; viva-voce.

orange, (sour ∼) aurantiaceous.

orangutan, pongid; simiid.

oration, (*obsolete*) concional, concionary.

oratory, declamatory; demegoric; epideictic, epidictic.

order, hierarchal, hierarchic; preceptive, preceptory; mandatory.

orgy, bacchanal, bacchanalian, bacchic; Dionysian; licentious; Saturnalian.

origin, archological; cosmogonic, cosmologic, cosmological; fontal; incipient; inchoate, inchoative; nascent; natal; native; principative, principle; (∼ of language) gluttogonic; (human ∼s) anthropogenic, anthropogenetic.

originality, primary, prime.

oriole, icterine.

Orkneys, Orcadian.

oscillation, fluctuable, fluctuant, fluctuous; vibrant, vibratory, vibrative.

ostentation, pedantic.

ostrich, ratite; struthious.

otter, lutrine; mustelid.

ounce, uncial.

outcast, Ishmaelitish.

outdoors, extraforaneous; hypaethral, hypethral; upaithric.

outgrowth, efflorescent.

oval, testiculate.

overflow, effusive; scaturient.

overhang, obumbrant.

overlap, imbricate; (numismatics) jugate.

owl, strigiform.

ownership, droitural, proprietorial.

ox, artiodactylous; bovine, bovoid.

ox-eye, boöpis.

Oxford, Oxonian.

oxygen, (lack of ∼) hypoxic.

oyster, asiphonate; ostracean, ostraceous, ostracine, ostreiform, ostreoid; (∼ eater) ostrephagous.

P

pacification, propitiable, propitial, propitiative.

paddlefish, chondrostean.

page, foliate.

pain, algesic, algetic; doloriferous, dolorific, dolorous; nociceptive; (∼ and pleasure) algedonic; (absence of ∼) analgesic, analgetic; (fear of ∼) algophobic, odynophobic; (love of ∼) algophilic; (producing ∼) algogenic.

paint, pastose.

painting, pictorial.

pair, didymous; jugate.

palate, (soft ∼) velar, velaric, veliform.

pale, albinic.

paleontology, fossilological.

pallor, blanching, blenching; sallow; wan.

palm, (of the hand) thenar, volar.

palm civet, paracoxurine.

palmistry, cheiromantic.

pan, patellate.

pangolin, manid.

pantheism, Xenophanean.

papal chair, gestatorial.

papaya, caricaceous.

paper, chartaceous; papyraceous.

paradise, ambrosial; Edenic; empyreal; heavenly; Hyperborean; idyllic; nirvanic; utopian.

parakeet, psittacine.

parallelism, paradromic.

paranoia, paraphrenic.

parasite, biophilous; endobiotic, epibiotic; epizoic; supercrescent.

parchment, Pergameneous; scrolar; vellumy.

pardon, exculpatory; venial.

parish, parochial.

parrot, psittaceous, psittacine.

parrot fish, oplegnathid.

part, fractional; particular, particularistic.

particle, atomic.

parting, discerptible; discretive; disjoined; disjunctive.

partridge, gallinaceous; perdicine.

party, factional, factionary, factious.

passion, ardent; calentural.

pastoral, bucolic.

pasture, pascual, pascuous.

patchwork, centonical.

path, (two ~s) bicursal.
patriot, chauvinistic.
pattern, archetypal, archetypical; normal, normative; paradigmatic.
pawnbroker, avuncular.
payment, alimonied; pensionary; redemptible, redemptional, redemptive, redemptorial, redemptory; salaried; stipendiary; (absence of ~) gratuitous.
pea, leguminiform, leguminose, leguminous; pisiform.
peace, Elysian; halcyon, halcyonian, halcyonic; irenic; pacific, pacifical, pacificatory; tranquil; quiescent.
peach, amygdalaceous; drupaceous.
peacock, pavonine.
peak, apical; epitomic, epitomical.
pear, malaceous; pyriform.
pearl, margaric; nacreous; perlaceous.
pebble, calculiform.
peccary, suid, suiform, suine; tayassuid.
pedigree, pedigraic.
peevishness, (Scottish) capernoited.
pelican, pelecanid, pelecaniform.
pelvis, (broad ~) platypellic.
penetration, perforate, perforative.
penmanship, chirographic, chirographical; (art of ~) calligraphic, calligraphical; (poor ~) cacographic, cacographical.
people, demotic; (fear of ~) anthropophobic, demophobic; (love of ~) philodemic.
pepper, piperaceous.
perception, discoverable; percipient; sagacious; sensible.
perfidy, (obsolete) disleal; treacherous.

perforation, foraminate, foraminous, foraminal; (two ~s) biforate.
peril, hazardous.
perimeter, circumferential.
periphery, circumscriptive.
periphrasis, circumlocutory; circumvolutory.
permanence, fixative; lasting.
permission, allowable.
perniciousness, scatheful.
perpendicularity, vertical.
Persian, Achaemenian.
persistence, assiduous; holdfast; inveterate; persevering; pertenacious, tenacious.
personality, characterologic, characterological; (slippery ~) saponaceous.
perspiration, sudoric; sudoriferous; (colored ~) chromidrotic; (foul-smelling ~) bromidrotic, osmidrotic; (producing ~) diaphoretic, hidrotic, sudorific.
persuasion, protreptic; psychagogic; suasible, suasive.
pet, cade.
petal, (absence of ~s) apetalous; (sharp ~) oxypetalous.
pettiness, chuck-farthing.
petrel, procellariiform, procellariid.
petrification, lapidescent.
petunia, solanaceous.
phalanger, petaurine.
phalanx, phalangiform; phalangeal.
phallus, aedeagal.
phantom, eidolic; (fear of ~s) spectrophobic.
Pharisee, Pharisaic.
pheasant, gallinaceous; phasianid, phasianoid.

phosphorescence, noctilucous; (~ on the sea) marfire.
pickerel, esociform.
picture, graphic; pictorial.
piece, fractional.
pig, artiodactylous; porcine; suiform, suine.
pigmentation, melanic, melanoid.
pika, lagomorphic.
pike, (fish) esociform.
pile, acervuline; cumulose.
pillage, depredatory; rapinic.
pillar, paxillar, paxillate, paxilliferous; columnar, columnal, columniform.
pimple, papular, papuliferous.
pine, coniferous.
pineal body, conarial.
pine tree, abietineous.
pinfeather, stipuliferous, stipuliform, stipular.
pinkness, damask.
pinnacle, zenith, zenithal.
pipe, fistulous, fistulose; tubular.
pit, abysmal, abyssal; foveate, foveiform, foveolate; lacunal, lacunary; glenoid.
pitch, (high ~) orthian; (tar) piceous.
pitcher, ascidiform; urceolate.
pity, pathetic, pathetical.
pivot, (joint) cyclarthroidal.
pixie, elfin, elfish.
place, local.
plagiarism, derivative.
plague, murrain; pestilent, pestilential.
plait, plicate.
plan, schematic.
plant, vegetational, vegetative; (~ dweller) phytophilous; (~ eater) herbivorous, phytophagous.

plantain, alismoid.
plastic, fictile.
Plata, (river) cisplatine.
plate, lamellar, lamelliform; laminar, laminose, lammate; placoid.
platypus, monotremal, monotrematous, monotremous.
plausibility, vraisemblable.
pleader, causidical.
pleasance, affable.
pleasure, agreeable; apolaustic; epicurean; hedonic, hedonistic; merry; sybaritic; voluptuous.
pledge, pignorate, pignoratitious.
plenty, abundant; Amalthean; cornucopian.
pliability, flexible, flexuous.
pliancy, limber.
plot, practitional.
plover, charadrine, charadrioid; pluvialine.
plow, (tax on a ~) carucal, carucated.
plowland, (tax) carucal, carucated.
plowshare, (*heraldry*) lavered.
plum, amygdalaceous; drupaceous; pruniform.
plunder, depredatory.
plutocracy, chrysocratic.
Po, (river) cispadane.
pocket gopher, geomyid.
pockmark, foveolate, foveolated.
point, acuminate, acuminulate; acute; cuspal, cuspate; cuspid, cuspidal, cuspidate; lanceolate, lanceolated; nibbed; punctate, punctiform, punctuate, punctulate; spiciform, spicigerous; styloid; subulate, subuliform; (two ~s) bicuspid, bicuspidate; (three ~s) tricuspid, tricuspidate.

pointlessness, vapid.

poison, attery; toxicologic, toxico-
logical; venomous; venenate;
(*archaic*) venenose; virose, virulent; (antidote for ∼) alexipharmic; (fear of ∼s) toxicophobic,
toxiphobic.

Poland, Polonian.

polish, vernicose.

pollen, gastrilegous; podilegous.

pollination, (∼ by beetles) can-
tharophilous; (∼ by insects) en-
tomophilous.

Polynesia, Nesogean.

pomegranate, balaustine.

pompano, carangid, carangoid.

pomposity, flatulent; bombastic.

pond, lagoonal; lacuscular.

pool, lacuscular.

pope, papal; (fear of ∼) papaphobic; (veneration of ∼) papolatrous.

poppy, papaveraceous.

populace, demotic.

popularity, celebrious.

population, larithmic.

porcupine, hystricid, hystricoid.

pore, ostiolar; porulose, porulous;
(small ∼) foraminulose.

porgy, sparoid.

porpoise, cetacean, cetaceous;
delphinoid.

porridge, pultaceous.

portend, ominous.

portico, narthecal; verandaed.

portion, particular, particularistic.

portliness, stout; obese; pinguid.

Portugal, Iberian, Iberic.

Portuguese man-of-war,
physalian.

possession, acquired, acquisite, ac-

quisitive; demesnial; oniomania-
cal.

postcard, deltiological.

posterior, retral; dorsal.

postulant, novitial.

potato, solanaceous.

potato beetle, chrysomelid.

potherb, oleraceous.

pottery, ceramic, ceramographic;
fictile.

pouch, bursiform; crumenal; marsupial; saccate, saccated; saccular,
sacculated; scrotiform.

pouring, effusive; libatory.

poverty, indigent; necessitous; penurious; ptochological; (fear of
∼) peniaphobic.

power, (great ∼) puissant.

practicality, banausic; pragmatic.

prairie, pratal.

praise, approbative, approbatory;
adulatory; encomiastic, encomias-
tical; eulogic, eulogious, eulogistic, eulogizing; laudable, laudative, laudatory; palmary;
panegyric, panegyrical; (∼ to
God) doxological.

prayer, orational.

precedence, prior.

precipice, (fear of ∼) cremnophobic.

precipitation, hyetal, hyetological.

precision, accurate; formal; veracious.

preclusion, obviable.

precursor, prodromal, prodromic.

predator, harpactophagous.

prediction, adumbrative; prolative.

preface, prolegomenal, prolegomenous.

preference, optative.

pregnancy, enceinte; gestatory; gravid; parous.

premise, hypothetical; theoretical.

preparation, propaedeutic.

presence, (grammatical ∼) adessive.

preservation, archival.

pretention, affected; ostentatious.

prevalence, regnant; predominant.

prevention, prophylactic.

prickle, acuate; aculeiform, aculeate; acuminate, acuminous; echinate; echinulate, echinuliform; spinoid, spinose, spinous.

prickly-pear cactus, opuntioid.

pride, arrogant, arrogative; Niobean; orgillous, orgulous; haughty; presumptuous; vainglorious.

priest, sacerdotal, sacerdotical.

primitiveness, protomorphic.

prince, (Persian ∼) satrapal, satrapic, satrapical.

prison, penal, penologic, penological.

pristineness, satyrine.

probability, acataleptic.

probity, (lack of ∼) dishonest.

procedure, actional.

procrastination, cunctatious, cunctative, cunctatory; dilatory.

production, effective, effectual; proliferant, proliferative, prolific, prolifical.

profit, beneficial; quaestuary; mercenary; remunerative, remuneratory.

profusion, plethoric.

progression, processional; progredient.

prohibition, verboten, forbidden.

projectile, ballistic.

projection, projicient; scarry; (∼ of the lower jaw) jimberjawed; (∼ of both jaws) prognathous, prognathic.

prolificacy, fertile.

promise, votal, votary, votive.

promptness, alacritous; punctual.

pronunciation, enunciative, enunciatory; (absence of ∼) aphonic; (correct ∼) orthoëpic, orthoëpical, orthoëpistic; (defective ∼) cacological; (incorrect ∼) cacoëpistic; (nonstandard ∼) paragogic, paragogical; (stammering ∼) traulistic.

proof, verifiable.

propaganda, agitprop.

property, demesnial.

prophecy, fatidic, fatidical; haruspical; oracular; prognosticative; pythonic; sibylic, sibylline; vatic, vatical, vaticinal, vaticinatory.

prophet, vatic; (killing of ∼) vaticidal.

prophetess, sibylline.

propriety, decorous.

prostitute, mertricious; pornographic.

protein, albuminoid, albuminous.

protoplasm, sarcodic.

protrusion, herniated.

protuberance, knobbed, knobby, knobular.

proverb, aphorismic, aphorismical, aphoristic; apothegmatic, apothegmatical; gnomic; maximistic; paroemiac, paroemiographical, paroemiological.

provocation, piquant.

proximity, (*rare*) propinquitous, propinquous.

prudery, pudibund; Victorian.
pruning knife, cultrate.
pseudorabies, (fear of ~) cynophobic, kynophobic.
psoriasis, psoric.
ptarmigan, tetraonid.
puberty, hebetic.
public, exoteric; popular; vulgar.
public finance, cameralistic.
publicity, (*archaic*) divulgatory.
publisher, editorial; redactorial.
pucker, bullate, bulliform.
puffbird, piciform.
puffer, (fish) tetraodont.
puffin, charadriiform.
pulley, trochlear, trochleate.
pulp, baccate.
pulsation, vibrant.
pulse, sphygmic, sphygmoid; (re-
cording of ~) sphygmographic,
sphygmographical; (slow ~)
bradycrotic.
pumpkin, cucurbitaceous.
pun, paronomastic.

punishment, mulctuary; penal, penological; (deserving ~) castigable.
pupil, discipular.
purchase, emptional; salable; venal.
purchasing, oniomaniac, oni-
omaniacal.
purgative, cathartic.
purification, depurative; lustral.
purity, intemerate. pristine; seraphic; virgin, virginal.
purpleness, porphyrous; Tyrian.
purplish black, sloe.
purpose, autotelic.
purposelessness, heterotelic.
pus, abscessed; purulent, puriform,
puruloid; pyogenic, pyogenous,
pyoid; suppurative, suppurant;
(formation of ~) pyopoietic.
pustule, (*archaic*) psydracious;
pimply.
pygmy, Lilliputian; midget.
python, boid.

Q

quahog, veneriform.
quail, gallinaceous, galliform; (button ∼) turnicine.
qualification, eligible.
qualm, scrupular, scrupulous.
quarrel, litigious.
quartz, jaspé, jaspered, jasperoid.
queen, monarchal, monarchial, monarchic; reginal.

question, rogatory.
questions and answers, catechetical.
quetzal, trogonoid.
quickness, volant; velocious, velocitous.
quicksand, (*archaic*) syrtic.

R

rabbit, lagomorphic; leporid; leporine, leporiform; (~'s foot) lagopous.

rabies, hydrophobic; lyssic.

raccoon, arctoidean.

race, ethnic, ethnical; gentilic; phyletic, phylogenic, phylogenetic, phylogenetical; (extermination of ~) genocidal; (government by ~) ethnocratic; (improvement of ~) eugenic; (yellow-skinned ~) xanthodermic.

racecourse, dromic.

radiance, auroral; effulgent, fulgent.

rage, furibund, furied, furious.

ragfish, icosteid, icosteine.

ragweed, ambrosiaceous.

railing, rabulistic, rabulous.

railroad, (fear of ~s) siderodromophobic.

rain, (rare) hyetological; ombrological; pluvial, pluviose, pluvious; (fear of ~) ombrophobic; (hater of ~) ombrophobus; (lacking ~) droughty, drouthy; (lover of ~) ombrophilous, ombrophilic; (measurement of ~) pluviographic, pluviometric, pluviometrical, udometric.

rainbow, iridian.

raising, arrect; (~ of young) nutricial.

ram, (~'s-head shape) arietinous.

rampart, circumvallate.

rancidity, reasty.

randomness, stochastic.

rank, hierarchal, hierarchic; serial.

rapidity, quick; alacritous.

rapture, ecstatic.

rarity, recherché.

rascal, picaresque.

rashness, temerarious, temeritous, temerous.

rasp, raduliform; cardiform.

rat, muriform, murine.

ratification, affirmative, affirmatory.

rationality, sane; sensible.

rattle, crepitant.

rattlesnake, crotalic, crotaline, crotaloid, crotaliform; solenoglyphic.

raven, corvoid.

ray, actinoid, actiniform.
reality, factitudinous; legitimate, legitime; noumenal; ontal; veridical.
realization, dispatchful; effectual, effectible, effective.
reappearance, atavistic.
rear, backward; postic, postical, posticous, posterior.
rearing, (*heraldry*) nampant.
reason, analytic; discoursive, discursive; rational.
reasoning, argumentative; dianoetic; noetic.
rebel, insurgent, mutine.
rebellion, insurrectionary, insurrectory.
rebirth, redivivus; renascent.
rebuffing, dismissive.
recency, neoteric.
reception, acceptable, acceptant, acceptive.
reciprocal, transmutual.
recitation, narratable, narrative, narratory.
recklessness, temerarious.
reclination, accumbent, recumbent; (*rare*) jacent.
recluse, anchoritic; eremitic; hermitic, hermitical, hermitish; pagurian.
reclusiveness, (*obsolete*) umbratic.
recognition, accredited; acknowledgeable, acknowledged.
recompensation, salaried.
record, archival.
recreation, leisurable, leisured.
rectitude, honest; upright; (lack of ∼) dishonest.
rectum, proctologic, proctological.
recumbency, (*rare*) jacent; prone.
recurrence, perennial; revenant.

redeeming, salvational.
redness, auburn; carmine; cinnabaric, cinnabarine; incarnadine; (*obsolete*) lac; erubescent, rubedinous, rubefacient, rubescent, rubicund, rubineous, rubious, rubricate, rubricose, rubrific; ruddy; rufescent; sanguine; vermilion; (fear of ∼) erythrophobic.
redstart, turdine.
redundancy, pleonastic.
reed, arundinaceous; baculiferous; calamiferous, calamiform; ferulaceous; fistulous.
reedbuck, reduncine.
refinement, elegant; polite, politeful; spirituel; (lack of ∼) vulgar.
reflection, advised; anacamptic; catoptric; mirrory; relucent; reverberative, reverberatory, reverbatory, reverberant; resonant; (∼ and refraction) catadioptric.
reflex, allokinetic.
reformation, resipiscent.
refraction, achromatic; anaclastic; dioptric; (∼ and reflection) catadioptric.
refreshment, refect, refectional, refectionary.
refrigeration, cryogenic; frigorific, frigoric.
refusal, dismissive; negative; recusant; reject, rejective.
refuse, colluvial; recremental; scoriac, scoriaceous, scoriform.
refutation, disprovable; elenctic.
region, epichoric.
register, archival; nomenclatorial, nomenclatural.

regularity, habitual, habituate; ordinal, ordinary; peloric; suant.
regulation, modulate; ordinant.
reign, regnal, regnant.
rejection, recusative; refusive, refutative, refutatory.
relation, agnate, agnatic; akin; analogical; consanguineous; sib, sibbed.
relationship, affinitive.
release, bailable; dischargeable.
relevance, *ad rem*; appropriate.
relief, acesodyne; anaglyphic; anodyne; coelanaglyphic; palliative.
reluctance, adverse.
remainder, residuary, residual.
remarkability, exceptional.
remedy, curative; panacean; therapeutic.
remittance, (*obsolete*) dispensable; payable.
remora, discocephalous.
remoteness, distal, distant.
removal, abstracted; dischargeable; displacive.
remuneration, profit.
renegade, apostate; tergiversatory, tergiverse.
renewal, recrudescent.
renouncement, disclamatory; dismissive.
renunciation, disclamatory.
repetition, battological; iterant; iterative; verbigerative; (~ of consonants) alliteral, alliterative.
replacement, displaceable, displacive.
reproduction, prolific; (sexual ~) amphigonic; (word for word ~) verbatim.
reptile, herpetic; herpetiform; herpetographical; herpetologic,

herpetological; (fear of ~s) herpetophobic, ophidiophobic.
repudiation, dismissive.
repugnance, antipathetic.
repulsion, disgustful, disgusting; rebarbative.
request, precatory; rogatory.
resemblance, pedomorphotic, pedomorphic.
resentment, envious; jealous; umbrageous.
reserve, shy; self-effacing; bashful.
residence, domiciliary.
resident, commorant.
resilience, elastic.
resin, guttiferous.
resistance, opposable, opposed, oppositional; renitent.
resonance, orotund; sonorous; syntonic; vibrating, vibrational, vibratory.
respect, deferential; venerable.
resplendence, bright; brilliant.
responsibility, liable; (fear of ~) hypengyophobic.
restlessness, erethic.
restoration, neoplastic.
restraint, abstemious.
restriction, coactive; limitative.
result, ecbatic.
reticence, secret, secretive.
retraction, palinodial.
retribution, nemesic.
return, remeant; retrograde.
revealing, heuristic.
revel, Bacchanalian; Dionysiac, Dionysian; dissolute; festive; orgiastic; Saturnalian.
revenue, bursal.
reverence, venerant, venerate, venerative.

reverie, visionary; dreamy.

reversal, backward; retrograde; retrogressive.

reversion, atavic, atavistic.

revocation, rescissory.

revolution, novation; sans-culottic.

rhea, ratite.

rhinoceros, ceratorhine; nasicorn.

rhumb line, loxodromic.

rhythm, cadenced.

rib, costal, costate, costated, costellate; laticostate.

ribbon, taeniform.

rice, riziform; (eater of ~) oryzivorous.

rickets, rachitic.

ridge, carinate; costate; lirate; varicellate.

ridicule, absurd.

rift, rimose.

right, dextral; (~ angle) orthogonal.

rigor, harsh.

rim, vallate.

ring, annular; torquate; (divination using ~s) dactyliomantic; (finger ~s) dactyliographic, dactyliologic; (interlocked ~s) gimmal; (signet ~) sphragistic.

ripple, undulant.

rise, acclivous.

rising, ascendant.

risk, jeopardous; parlous.

rite, sacral, sacramental, sacramentary.

ritual, ceremonialistic; formulistic; rubricistic.

river, potamic, potamologic, potamological; fluvial, fluviatile, fluviatic, fluminose; (~ bottom) subfluvial; (~ dweller) fluvicoline; (fear of ~s) potamophobic.

riverbank, riparian; (~ dweller) ripicolous.

roach, blattid.

roadrunner, cuculid.

robber fly, brachycerous.

robe, vestural.

robin, turdoid.

rock, brecciated; (rare) lithoidological; rupicolous, rupestrine, rupestral, rupestrian; saxicolous; (divination using ~s) lithomantic; (drawings on ~s) petroglyphic; (living among ~s) lithodomous, petricolous, petrophilous, saxicoline, saxigenous; (worship of ~s) lithoidolatrous.

rod, bacilliform, bacillary; baculine, baculiform; rhabdoid; virgate, virgulate.

rodent, gliriform.

rogue, picaresque.

rope, funiform.

roller, (~ bird) coraciform.

romanticism, quixotic.

Rome, (ancient ~) togate.

roof, cleithral; tectiform.

root, radical, radicose, radicular, radiculose; rhizomic, rhizoid, rhizomorphic, rhizomorphoid, rhizomorphous; (~ eater) rhizophagous; (~ dweller) radicicolous.

ropewalker, funambulic.

rorqual, (whale) balaenopterid.

rotary, trochilic; verticillary, vertiginous.

rotifer, notommatid.

roughness, boisterous; churlish, churly; knock-about; knock-me-

down; robustious; squarrose,
squarrulose; surly.

roundness, disciform; discoid, dis-
coidal.

roundworm, ascarid.

row, serial; tiered.

royalty, majestic, regal.

rubbish, detrital.

ruddiness, rubicund.

rudeness, boisterous; boorish;
brutish; carlish; discourteous;
surly.

ruin, pernicious.

ruler, dynastic, dynastical; monarchial, monarchic.

running, cursive, cursorial.

ruralism, arcadian; bucolic,
bucolical; georgic; idyllic; pastoral; rustic.

rush, (plant) juncaceous;
junciform.

rust, (color) ferruginous; rubiginous.

rusticity, boorish; geoponic.

S

S, (∼-shape) sigmoid, sigmoidal.
Sabbath, Sabbatarian, Sabbatic,
Sabbatical.
saber-toothed tiger, machaer-
odont, machairodont.
sable, zibeline.
sac, thecal, thecate; (small ∼)
sacculate; (sperm ∼) spermathe-
cal.
sacredness, hierologic, hierologi-
cal; (fear of ∼) hierophobic.
sacrifice, oblate, oblational, obla-
tionary, oblatory; piacular.
sacristy, vestiary.
saddle, sellate.
sadism, algolagnic.
sadness, disconsolate, discontent;
dispirited.
safety, salvatory.
sagacity, omniscient; perspicacious;
prescient; sapient, sapiential;
shrewd.
sail, velamentous, velic, veliferous.
sailfish, istiophorid.
saint, hagiologic; hagiological; (hatred of ∼s) hagiophobic; (lives
of ∼s) hagiographic; (worship of
∼s) hagiolatrous.

salad, acetarious.
salamander, cryptobranchid.
salary, emolumental.
sale, auctionary; vendible.
salt, alkalescent, alkali, alkaline, al-
kaloid; halinous, haloid; saline,
salvific; soterial.
saltwater, brack, brackish, bracky.
salvation, soteriological.
sand, arenaceous, arenarious, are-
noid, arenose; sabellan, sabuline,
sabulous; tophaceous; psammologic; psammous; (∼ dweller)
ammophilous, arenicolous, psammophilous, psammophytic.
sand dollar, clypeastroid.
sandgrouse, pteroclid.
sandpiper, charadrine, charadrioid;
scolopaceous.
sarcasm, mordacious, vitriolic.
sardine, clupeid.
sassafras, lauraceous.
satire, Aristophanic; goliardic;
parodistic; sillographic.
Saturday, sabbatine, sabbatical.
Saturn, Cronian.
satyr, capripedal, capripedic.

saucer, patelliform.
sausage, (∼ shape) allantoid, allantoidal; botuliform.
savage, fiendish, fierce.
saw, serrate, serrated, serratic, serriform.
sawdust, scobicular, scobiform.
sawfish, batoid; pristid.
sawfly, tenthredinid; terebrant.
saxifrage, grossulariaceous.
scab, escharotic.
scale, (*heraldry*) escalloped; furfuraceous, furfurous; laminable, laminar, laminary, laminate, laminated, laminose; leprose; scabbed, scabby, scabrescent, scabrous; squamate, squamous, squamulose; squamiform; squarrose, squarrous, squarrulose; urostegal.
scallop, crenate; (∼ shell) pectiniform.
scandal, flagitious.
Scandinavia, Nordic.
scar, cicatricial, cicatricose; cicatrose, cicatrisate, cicatrizate; escharotic; hiliferous; uloid; (promote formation of a ∼) cicatrisive, cicatrizant.
scarlet fever, scarlatinal.
scazon, choliambic; Hipponactean.
scent, aromatic; odorate, odoriferant, odoriferous, odorific; redolent.
scholar, discipular; philomathean, philomathic, philomathical.
schoolmaster, pedantic.
science, mathetic.
scimitar, acinaciform.
scissors, (∼ shape) forficiform, forcipiform, forcipulate.

scorn, derisive, derisory; haughty; sardonic.
scorpion, pedipalpous.
scorpion fish, scleropareiceous.
Scotland, Caledonian.
scoundrel, villainous.
scrape, (*archaic*) excoriate.
scraper, cardiform; raduliform.
screw, spiroid; helic, helical; spiral.
scribe, sopheric.
scroll, turbinate; volute, voluted, volutiform.
scrotum, oscheal.
scurvy, scorbutic.
scythe, falciform, falcate, falcular.
sea, cismarine; (*obsolete*) haliographic; marine, marinal; oceanic, oceanographic, oceanographical; pelagic; Poseidonian; thalassic, thalassographic, thalassographical; (∼ dweller) maricolous; (fear of the ∼) thalassophobic.
sea anemone, actinian, actiniform.
sea cucumber, holothurian; synaptid.
sea horse, hippocampine.
seagull, laroid.
seal, (animal) phocine; (signet) obsignatory; sigillate, sigillated, sigillary, sigillative, sigillistic, sigillographical; sillographic; sphragistic.
sea lily, crinoid, crinoidal.
seam, commissural; sutural.
Sea of Marmara, Propontic.
search, expiscatory; scrutinous; zetetic.
seashore, littoral; coastal; orarian.
sea urchin, cidarid; echinal, echinoid, echinoderm, echinoderma-

tous, echinodermic; (fossil ~) echinital.

seaweed, algoid, algous; fucoid, fucoidal, fucous; (~ eater) fuciphagous.

seclusion, private; umbratic; cloistral; recluse; sequestral.

secrecy, clancular; clandestine.

secret, arcanal, arcane; epoptic; hugger-mugger.

secretion, salival, salivary, salivous; secernment; sialoid, sialic.

secularity, laic.

seed, seminiferous, seminific; spermic; (~ eater) granivorous, seminivorous; (having two ~s) dispermous.

seer, medianic, medianimic.

segment, meristic; merogenetic.

seizure, rapacious; usurpative.

selection, analectic; assortative; co-optative; eclectic, eclectical; pericopal, pericopic.

self, autological; (~-awareness) coenesthetic, cenesthetic; (~-deprivation) ascetic; (~-digestion) autolytic; (~-fertilization) autogamic; (~-generated) autogenous; (~-government) autarkic, autarkical; autocephalous; (~-interest) introvertive, introversive; (~-knowledge) autognostic; (~-love) autophilic; (loss of ~-possession) disconcerted, disconcerting; (fear of being by one~) autophobic, eremiophobic, eremophobic, monophobic; (killing one~) suicidal; (worship of ~) autolatrous, egolatrous.

selling, vendible.

semen, seminiferous, seminific.

sense, (vital ~) coenesthetic, cenesthetic.

sense organ, organoleptic.

sensibility, (absence of ~) stolid.

sensitivity, aeschynomenous; nervish, nervous.

sentimentality, bathetic; maudlin, mawkish; Wertherian.

separateness, discerptible; discretive; disjoinable.

separation, analytic; severable, severed; (violent ~) divulsive.

sequin, diamanté.

seriousness, earnest; grave; severe, severish; solemn.

sermon, homiletic, homiletical; (hatred of ~s) homilophobic.

serpent, herpetiform; reptilian; ophic; (fear of ~s) herpetophobic.

servant, menial.

service, beneficial; voluntary.

servility, obsequious, (*obsolete*) obsequent; sycophantic, sycophantical, sycophantish; vassaled; vernile.

set, systematic.

setting, fixative; scenic.

settlement, adjudicative.

seven, septenary; septimal; septuple, septuplicate; (~ -day period) heptal, hebdomadal; (~ -sided figure) heptagonal, heptahedral.

severity, acrimonious; acerb; Draconic, Draconian.

sewer, cloacal.

sex, carnal; (fear of ~) coitophobic, cypridophobic, erotophobic, genophobic; (having two ~es) amphierotic, androgynous, hermaphroditic, monoecious, synoecious; (sadomasochistic ~) algolagnic.

sexuality, gamic.

shad, clupeid.

shade, adumbral; umbrageous, umbriferous, umbral, umbrous.

shadow, adumbral; adumbrant, adumbrative; sciagraphic, skiagraphic; umbrageous, umbriferous, umbral, umbratic, umbratile, umbrous; (dispelling of ~s) scialytic (long ~) macroscian.

shaft, scapiform, scapoid.

shame, inglorious.

shank, crural.

shark, galeiform; (fear of ~s) galeophobic; (maneater ~) carcharodont; (tiger ~) carcharinid.

sharpness, acrid; acronarcotic; acuate.

shave, depilatory.

Shaw, George Bernard, Shavian.

shearwater, procellariiform, procellariid.

sheath, vaginal, vaginate; (absence of ~) alemmal.

shedding, deciduous; ecdysial; exuviable.

sheen, nitid.

sheep, artiodactylous; ovine; (~ skin) vervecine.

sheet, lamellar, lamelliform; laminar, laminose, laminate.

shell, bosselated; carapacic; conchate, conchiform, conchitic, conchiferous, conchyliferous, conchological; nautiliform; testaceous; (snail ~) cochleate, cochleiform.

shelter, nidulant.

shepherd, bucolic; pastoral.

sheriff, shrieval.

shield, clypeolar, clypeate, clypeated, clypeiform; scutal; (~ shape) scutate, scutiform, scutatiform.

shin, cnemial.

shinbone, cnemial; tibial.

shine, relucent; rutilant; vernicose.

shiner, cyprinid, cyprinoid.

shining, bright, brilliant; effulgent, profulgent; nitid; splendent.

ship, naval, navicular, naviform.

shipworm, teredinid.

shipwreck, (*obsolete*) naufragous.

shirt, (*Scottish*) sarkit.

shiver, palpitant.

shoe, saboted; shod; calced.

shore, littoral; (~ dweller) limicoline.

shorthand, brachygraphic; stenographic.

shortness, abbreviate; brief; decurtate.

shoulder, axillant, axillar, axillary; humeral; (~ blade) scapular, scapulary.

showiness, garish; gaudy.

showing off, orchidaceous.

shrew, (animal) soricine; (woman) termagant, viraginous.

shrewdness, adroit; callid; perspicacious; sagacious; yankee.

shrimp, caridean, caridoid; macrural, macruran, macruroid.

Shropshire, Salopian.

shroud, sindological.

shrub, arbuscular; bushy; frutescent, fruticose.

shrub-shaping, topiary.

shyness, Daphnean; diffident; humilific; (*Scottish*) skeigh.

sickbed, clinic.

sickle, falciform, falcate, falcular.

sickness, ailing; languent, languescent; languid, languishing; (*rare*) maladive; nauseous; valetudinarian; (green ∼) chlorotic.

side, lateral; (thick ∼) pachystichous; (one ∼) unilateral, unilineal; (two ∼s) bilateral; (three ∼s) trilateral; (four ∼s) quadrilateral; (five ∼s) pentagonal; (six ∼s) hexagonal; (seven ∼s) heptagonal; (eight ∼s) octagonal; (nine ∼s) nonagonal; (ten ∼s) decagonal; (eleven ∼s) hendecagonal; (twelve ∼s) dodecagonal.

sieve, cribrose, cribral, cribrate, cribriform.

sigh, suspirious.

sight, visible, visual.

sight and hearing, oculauditory.

sign, semiologic, semiological; semiotic, semiotical, semeiotic, semeiotical.

signet, sigillary; (∼ ring) sphragistic.

sign language, dactylologic.

silence, aphonic, (*rare*) conticent; taciturn.

silk, byssoid, byssine, byssiferous; massaline; sericate, sericated, sericeous; sericultural.

silk-screen printing, serigraphic.

silkworm, (∼ moth) bombycid, bombycine; quadrivoltine; sericultural.

silver, argent, argental, argenteous, argentine, argentiferous, argentous.

silverfish, lepismid, lepisosteid.

similarity, alike; analogical; kindred; like.

simplicity, naive; stupid.

sin, hamartiological; peccable, peccant; piacular; transgressional, transgressive, transgredient; (fear of ∼) hamartophobic, peccatiphobic, peccatophobic.

sincerity, earnest; genuine; pectoral; whole-hearted.

singer, cantatory.

singing, cantative, cantatory; (∼ of birds) cantoral, cantorous.

single-mindedness, monomaniacal.

Sioux, Abanic.

Sirius, canicular; cynic; Sothic.

sister, sororal, sororial; (∼ killing) sororicidal.

sitting, sessional.

six, senary; sexenary; sextuple, sextuplex, sextuplicate; sexpartite.

sixty, sexagesimal.

skate, (fish) raiiform.

skeleton, (ape ∼) pithecometric; (bony ∼) osteal; (coral ∼) coenosteal.

skeptic, agnostic; (*obsolete*) aporetic.

skepticism, pyrrhonian.

sketch, delineative.

skill, adept; daedal, daedalian; enginous; habile; handy; practic, practical; (*obsolete*) solert.

skin, cutaneous; (*rare*) cutaneal; cuticular, cutigerous; dermal, dermatic, dermatoid, dermoid; dermatological; (shedding of ∼) exuvial; (∼ thickening) pachymenic; (dark ∼) melanian, melanic, melanochroous; mela-

nodermic; (thick ∼)
pachydermic, pachydermatous;
(thin ∼) pellicular, pelliculate;
percutaneous; subcutaneous.

skink, scincoid, scincidoid.

skull, cranial, craniate; craniological; (∼ conformation) phrenological; (flat ∼) chamecephalic,
chamecephalous; (long ∼)
dolichocranic; (measurement of
∼) craniometric, craniometrical,
cranioscopic, cranioscopical;
(primitive ∼) archaecraniate.

skunk, mustelid.

sky, celestial; (*obsolete*) celestine;
coelar; empyreal, empyrean; sub-
aerial; supernal.

slab, tabular.

slackness, flaccid; limp.

slag, scoriform, scoriac, scoriaceous.

slander, aspersive; calumnious;
maledicent, maledictive, maledictory; obliquious; vilipend.

slate, schistaceous.

slave, gallerian; (rule by ∼s)
dulocratic.

slavery, mancipative; servile.

sleep, dormant, dormient; lethargic; morphean; narcoleptic;
noddy; slumbering, slumberous;
somnial, somniative, somnifacient, somniferous, somnific,
somnify, somniloquent, somnolent; soporific, soporiferous; (∼
learning) hypnopedic; (fear of
∼) hypnophobic.

sleeplessness, (*rare*) insomnious,
insomnolent.

sleepwalking, noctambulic, noctambulous, noctambulant,
noctambulistic; somnambulant,

somnambulistic; (∼ in moon-
light) lunambulistic.

slenderness, gracile; (becoming
slender) gracilescent.

slime, blennoid; glairy; limous; (∼
mold) myxomycetous.

sling, fundiform.

slip, labile.

slipper, calceiform; sandaliform;
soleiform.

slipperiness, lubric, lubricate, lu-
bricative, lubricatory, lubricous.

slope, (downward ∼) declinate,
declivitous, declivous; (upward
∼) acclivitous.

sloth, xenarthral; edentate; (*obsolete*) thokish.

slowness, laconic; laggard.

slug, limacine, limacoid.

sluggishness, languid, languescent.

slyness, (*rare*) subdolous.

smallness, diminutive; Lilliputian;
miniature.

smallpox, variolate, variolous, varioloid; varioliform.

smell, aromatic; fetid; malodorous;
mephitic; nasute; nidorous; olfactory; osphretic; osmetic; redolent;
savored, savory; (fear of ∼s) olfactophobic.

smog, miasmic.

smoke, fuliginous; (*obsolete*) fumid;
(divination using ∼) capnoman-
tic, empyromantic; (hatred of ∼)
misocapnic.

smoking, fumacious; fumatory.

smoothness, jarless; levigate; mellifluous; polite, politeful.

snake, anguiform; colubrine,
colubroid; diapsidan; elapid,
elapine, elapoid; ophidian,
ophidic; ophiographic, ophio-

logic, ophiological; peropodous;
reptilian; serpentiform, serpentine, serpentinoid; viperiform;
(∼ eater) ophiophagous; (divination using ∼s) ophiomantic;
(fear of ∼s) ophidiophobic;
(worship of ∼s) ophiolatrous.
snapper, (fish) lutjanid.
snapping turtle, chelydroid.
sneeze, sternutatory; errhine.
snipe, (bird) charadrine,
charadrioid.
snook, centropomid.
snoring, stertorous.
snout, (narrow ∼) angustirostrate.
snow, nival, niveous; (∼ dweller)
nivicolous; (∼ blindness) chionableptic.
soap, saponaceous, saponary, saponifiable.
soaring, (∼ in spirit) essorant.
softening, detumescent.
softness, malacotic; mollescent.
soil, agrological; alluvial, alluvious;
earthy; edaphic; pedologic, pedo-
logical; (∼ dweller) geophilous;
(∼ eater) geophagous.
sole, (fish) anacanthous; (foot)
plantar, volar.
solemnity, earnest; serious; severe,
severish.
solitude, hermitic, hermitical; eremitic; infrasocial; single.
son, filial.
sonority, canorus.
soot, fuliginous.
soothing, hesychastic.
soothsayer, haruspical.
sophistication, urbane.
sorcery, apotropaic; (*archaic*)
goetic, goetical; jujuistic; necro-

mantic; sorcerous, sortilegic, sortilegious; theurgic, theurgical;
veneficious, venenate, venene.
sore, lazarly, lazarous.
sorrow, grievous; languorous; lamentable, lamentational, lamentatory, lamented, lamentive;
luctiferous; pathetic, pathetical;
plaintive; sad.
soul, psychic, psychical; (manifestation of ∼) psychorrhagic;
(transmigration of ∼s) metempsychic, metempsychosic, metempsychosical; (unity of ∼s)
monopsychic, monopsychical.
sound, crepitant; noiseful, noisy;
onomatopoeic, onomatopoetic,
onomatopoietic; phonetic, phonetical, phonic; phonogramic,
phonogrammic; sonal, sonic; (absence of ∼) aphonic; (harmonious ∼) euphonic, euphonical,
euphonious; (harsh ∼) cacophonic, cacophonous, strident,
stridulous; (reflector of ∼) phonocamptic.
source, fontal; principle.
sourness, acerb, acerbic; acetic,
acetose, acetous; acid; (*obsolete*)
pontic; vinegary.
south, austral; meridional.
South Pole, antarctic.
sovereign, regnal.
sovereignty, (absolute ∼) autarchic, autarchical; autocratic; des-
potic; dictatorial; monarchal, monarchial; totalitarian.
space, lacunal, lacunary; (fear of
open ∼s) agoraphobic, ceno-
phobic, kenophobic.
Spain, Hispanic; Iberian, Iberic.

Spanish fly, cantharidal, cantharidian.

spar, spathic, spathose; foliated; lamellar.

sparkle, bright; brilliant; scintillant, scintillescent, scintillose, scintillous.

sparrow, passerine, passeriform.

spasm, (muscular ∼) clonic.

spathe, spadiceous, spadicose.

speaker, orational; oratorical, oratoric; Demosthenean, Demosthenian, Demosthenic; declamatory; rhetorical; bombastic.

spear, hastate.

species, phyletic.

speck, variolitic.

speckle, jasper, jasperated; mottled.

spectacle, pageant, pageanted, pageantic.

speech, articulate, articulative; logographic; utterance; verbomotor; (∼ defect) logopedic.

speechmaking, demegoric; (sacred ∼) homiletic, homiletical; (vain ∼) mataeological.

speed, velocious, velocitous; celeritous; alacritous.

spelling, orthographic; (incorrect ∼) cacographic, cacographical; (phonetic ∼) phonographic, phonographical.

sphere, globose, globular, globous; orbicular.

sphinx, sphingine.

spider, arachnid, arachnoid; araneiform; arthropodal, arthropodan; attid; (fear of ∼s) arachnephobic; (tubular ∼ web) tubicolous.

spike, spiciform, spicigerous; (many ∼s) polystachyous.

spinal cord, myeloid, myelonic.

spindle, fusiform, fusid; clostridial, clostridian.

spine, acanthoid, acanthous; echinate, echinulate, echinuliform; hispid; hyperchordal; myelic; paxillar, paxillate, paxilliferous; rachiform; vertebral, vertebrate, vertebrated, vertebriform.

spinning, Minervic; strobic.

spinster, discovert.

spiral, gyratory, gyrous; helical, helicine, helicoid; spiriform; turbinate; volute.

spirit, galliard; (absence of ∼) lack-fettle; phlegmatic.

spirit-rapping, typtological.

spirits, (fear of ∼) demonophobic.

spite, contumelious; knappish; splenetic; vicious.

spitting, expectorant; (∼ of blood) hemoptoic.

spleen, splenetic, splenic; lienal.

splendor, bright; brilliant; gallant; galloptious; grand; majestic; orgulous.

split, disruptured; fissile; rimose; scissile.

spokes, verticillate.

sponge, (∼ dweller) spongicolous.

spoon, cochlear; cochleariform.

spore, (∼ case) thecal, thecate; vaginiferous.

spot, liturate; macular, maculate, maculated, maculose; naevoid; punctate, punctiform, punctuate, punctulate; (eyelike ∼) ocellar, ocellation; (hard ∼) callous, callose; (marked with ∼s) irrorate.

spouse, sponsal.

spread, patulous.
sprightliness, brisk.
spring, (∼ dweller) fontinal; (season) vernal; (flourishing in ∼) vernant.
sprout, germinant.
spruce, abietineous.
square, boxy; piazzaed; quadrate, quadratic, quadratical.
squash, cucurbitaceous.
squash bug, coreid.
squatness, fodgel.
squirrel, sciuromorphic; (flying ∼) sciuropteric; (ground ∼) sciurid, sciuroid, sciurine.
stage, histrionic; scenic.
stain, neutrophile; slubbering, slubbery; stigmal; tinctorial.
stake, (small ∼) paxillose; palar.
stalk, peduncular; petiolate; stipiform, stipital, stipitate.
stamen, allagostemonous.
stamp, empaistic; philatelic, philatelical, philatelist, philatelistic; sigilated.
standard, normal, normative.
standing, orthostatic.
star, astral; astriferous; astrologic, astrological, astrologous; astronomical; sidereal; stellar, stelliferous, stellular, stellulate; (divination using ∼s) astromantic, sideromantic; (fear of ∼s) siderophobic; (mapping of ∼s) astrographic, uranographic; (measurement of ∼s) astrometric, astrometrical; (rising or setting ∼) acronical, acronichal, acronyc, acronycal, acronych, acronychal, acronyctous.
starch, amyliferous.
star coral, astraean.

starvation, marasmic, marasmous, marantic; marasmoid.
starfish, asteroidean, (basket ∼) euryalid.
starling, sturnine, sturnoid, sturniform.
statistics, demographic, demographical.
stealing, brigandish; kleptomaniacal; plagiaristic; (fear of ∼) kleptophobic.
steepness, brant.
stem, cauliform, caulomic; peduncular; scapiform, scapoid; (succulent ∼) chylocaulous.
stench, fetid; graveolent; malodorant, malodorous; mephitic; nidorous; noisome.
stepmother, novercal.
sterility, acarpous; aseptic; axenic; otiose.
sternness, austere; severe, severish.
sticking, adherent; adhesional, adhesive; viscid; viscous.
stiffness, anchylotic, ancylotic, ankylotic.
stifling, strangulative; suffocating, suffocative.
stillness, stagnant.
stimulus, allassotonic.
sting, aculeate; urticant.
stingray, masticurous.
stirrup, (∼ of the ear) stapedial.
stitch, (∼ like mark) consute; (done by ∼ing) sutile.
stolidity, stupid.
stomach, cardiac, cardiacal; gastric, gastrological; ventricular.
stone, lithic, lithoid, lithoidal; rupestral, rupestrian; (∼ dweller) lapidicolous; (∼ painting)

lithochromic; (~ printing) lithographic.

stone age, (earliest ~) archaeolithic, eolithic, protolithic.

stork, ciconiform, ciconine; grallatorial.

storm, nimbiferous, nimbose; procellous.

straight line, rectigrade, rectilinear.

straightness, vertilinear.

strangeness, eccentric, eccentrical; unfamiliar.

stranger, alien.

strap, cingulate; lingulate.

stratification, varved.

straw, stramineous.

strawberry, rosaceous.

streak, vittate.

stream, fluvial, fluviatic, fluviatile; (~ dweller) autopotamic, fluvicoline; (between ~s) interfluvial.

strength, Achillean; athletic; Atlantean; boisterous; bracing; herculean; mighty; nervish, nervous; puissant; roborant; Samsonic, Samsonistic; sthenic; stout; vigorous.

stress, accentual; metrical; ictic.

stretching, elastic.

strictness, severe, severish.

stripe, bandy; taeniate; vittate.

strophe, strophaic.

structure, edificable, edificatory, edificial.

stubbornness, adamant; bullheaded; calcitrant, recalcitrant; froward; intractable; intransigent; obdurate; pervicacious; refractory.

student, discipular.

stunning, stupefacient, stupefied.

stunt, aerobatic.

stupidity, addlebrained; addlepated; anserine; asinine; assish; backward; blunt, bluntish; calvish; oscitant; thimblewitted.

stupor, carotic; narcose; stupefacient.

sturgeon, acipenserid, acipenserine; chondrostean.

stuttering, dysarthric.

subalpine, (~ dweller) orophilous.

subdean, subdecanal.

submission, acquiescent; obsequent, obsequious; yieldable, yielding.

substance, (lack of ~) disembodied.

substitution, ersatz; euphemistic; succedaneous; vicarious.

subterrain, hypogeal.

succession, subalternating.

succulence, juicy.

sucker, haustellate, haustorial.

sucking, lactant.

suction, vacuum.

Sudan, Nigritian.

suddenness, abrupt.

suet, stearic.

suffering, agonized; grievous; pathic.

sufficience, adequate, adequative.

suffix, afformative; hypocoristic.

suffocation, apneic, apnoeic.

sugar, sacchariferous.

suicide, Kamikaze.

suitability, eligible; habile; idoneous.

sulfur, thionic.

summation, perorational, perorative, peroratory.

summer, canicular; estival; (late ~) serotinal.

summit, apical.

sumptuousness, lautitious; opiparous.

sun, aphelian; heliac, heliacal, heliocentric; solar, soliform; (fear of ~) heliophobic; (measurement of ~) heliographic, heliographical; (setting ~) occasive; (worship of ~) heliolatrous.

Sunday, dominical.

sundew, droseraceous.

sundial, gnomonic; sciatheric.

sunfish, moloid.

sunlight, (~ dweller) heliophilous.

superficiality, sophomoric.

superiority, elder, eldest; excellent; palmary.

supper, coenaculous.

supplement, accessorial; added, additive, additory; adscititious.

suppleness, flexible, flexuous; leathwake.

supplication, obsecrationary, obsecratory; precative, precatory.

support, (heraldry) accosted; pedimental, pedimented.

suppression, quellable.

surface, areal.

surf clam, mactroid.

surgery, chirurgic, chirurgical; (fear of ~) tomophobic.

surpassing, frabjous.

surprise, astonishing; obreptitious.

surveying, gromatic.

susceptibility, allergic; diathetic.

suspicion, querulous.

sustenance, papular, pabulary, pabulous.

swallow, (bird) hirundine.

swallowing, deglutitious, deglutitory; (~ difficulty) dysphagic.

swamp, maremmatic; quashy; (~ dweller) uliginous.

swan, cygnine.

sweat, exudative, exudatory; hidrotic; sudorific, sudoriparous; (~ gland) syringadenous.

sweeping, rasant.

sweet clover, melilotic.

sweetness, sauveolent.

sweet potato, convolvulaceous.

swelling, edematous; intumescent; torose, torulose; tuberous; (rare) turgent; turgescent, turgid; varicose, varicosed, varicosity.

swimming, natant, natatorial, natatorious, natatory.

swine, porcine.

swineherd, sybotic.

swirl, vortical, vorticose.

switch, ferulic.

Switzerland, Helvetian, Helvetic.

sword, gladiate; rapiered; xiphoid.

swordfish, xiphioid.

sycophant, gnathonic.

syllable, acatalectic; (two ~s) disyllabic; (three ~s) trisyllabic; (four ~s) quadrasyllabic; (five ~s) pentasyllabic; (excess ~s) perissosyllabic.

symbiote, endobiotic.

symbol, allusive; aniconic; semiotic.

symmetry, actinomorphic; allochiral; pleorian, pleoriate, pleoric.

sympathy, humane; kindhearted.

syntax, solecistic.

syphilis, luetic.

T

table, mensal; tabular; (∼ conversation) deipnosophistic.

taffeta, tabby.

tail, caudal; cercal; caudate, caudated; (∼ like) caudiform; (absence of ∼) acaudal, ecaudate; (long ∼) macrurous; (two ∼s) bicaudal.

tailor, sartorial, sartorian.

taking, adoptable.

talent, aptitudinal.

talisman, telesmatic.

talk, babblative, babblesome, babbling; loquacious; sermonic; (fear of ∼ing) laliophobic, lalophobic.

talkativeness, garrulous; glib; logorrheic; verbose; voluble.

tallow, sebaceous.

tamarin, callithricid.

taming, (absence of ∼) feral.

tangency, sextactic.

tangle, (*obsolete*) implicate; tatty; tauted.

tanning, scytodepsic.

taper, subulate.

tapestry, arrased.

tapeworm, cestodan, cestoid; (∼ destroyer) taeniacidal.

tapir, pachydermoid, pachydermatoid.

tarantula, theraphosid.

tardiness, late, latesome, latish.

tarsier, lemuroid.

tartness, acidy.

Tasmanian devil, dasyurid.

taste, elegant; gustable, gustative; palatable; sapid, saporific, saporous; savory; (fear of ∼) geumophobic.

tattler bird, scolopacine.

taunting, sarcastic, sarcastical.

tax, ad valorem; fiscal; leviable.

taxation, assessorial, assessory.

teaching, didactic; educable, educatable; inculcatory; pedagogic; pedantic.

tear, (rip) lacerable; lacerant; lacerated; lacerative.

teardrop, lacrimoid, lacrimiform; lachrymal, lacrimal.

tearing, aflow.

tedium, boring, borish.

teeming, gushing.

teetotaler, nephalistic.

temper, (bad ∼) atrabilious, atrabiliar.

temperament, disposed.
temperance, abstemious; ascetic.
tempo, agogic.
temporariness, ad interim.
ten, decadic; decamerous; decimal; decuple; denary.
tenacity, gripple; holdfast; persistent; pertinaceous.
tenant, lairdly.
tendency, adient.
tenderloin, psoatic.
tenderness, fond.
tendon, desmoid.
tendril, capreolate; cirrous.
tentacle, (absence of ~s) acerous.
tenure, feudal, feudalistic, feudatorial.
tepidness, lew.
termite, (fear of ~s) eisoptrophobic, isopterophobic.
tern, larid.
terra cotta, (color) testaceous.
territory, demesnial; regional, regionary, regioned.
testator, legatorial.
Teuton, gothonic.
Thames, (north of the ~) cispontine.
theater, histrionic; Thespian.
theft, furacious; larcenic, larcenish, larcenous.
theology, patrologic, patrological.
thespian, actorish, actory.
thickening, pachyntic.
thicket, bosky; bushy.
thickness, broad; turbid.
thief, kleptic, kleptistic; kleptomaniac; (fear of thieves) cleptophobic, kleptophobic.
thievery, Cyllenian.
thigh, femoral.

thinness, attenuate; ectomorphic; gracile; lank, lanky; scarious; wafery.
13, (fear of number ~) tridecaphobic, triskaidekaphobic.
thistle, carduaceous; cynaraceous, cynaroid.
thorn, spinous.
thought, cogitative; dianoetic; ruminative; speculative.
thoughtfulness, cogitabund, cogitabundous.
thoughtlessness, incogitant.
thousand, chiliadal, chiliadic.
thousandth, millesimal.
thread, catenulate; filiform; nemaline; quadrifilar.
threat, comminatory, minatorial, minatory.
three, trinal, trinary, trine; tripartite.
threshhold, liminal, liminary.
throat, guttural; jugular.
throng, celebrious.
throwback, atavic, atavistic.
throwing, jaculatorial.
thrush, muscicapine.
thrust, jabbing.
thumb, pollical.
thunder, (rare) brontological; (~ and lightning) fulmineous, fulminous; (divination using ~) keraunomantic, ceraunomantic, keraunoscopic; (fear of ~) brontophobic, keraunophobic, ceraunophobic, tonitrophobic, tonitruphobic.
Tiahuanaco, epigonal, epigonic.
tick, acarian, acaridan.
tide, neap.
tidyness, natty.

tile, tegular.

tillage, aratory; geoponic, geoponical.

tilt, acock.

time, chronal; chronologic, chronological; chronic; (*obsolete*) chronical; proleptical; (coincidence in ∼) synchronistic, synchronistical; (fear of ∼) chronophobic; (historical ∼) diachronic; (measurement of ∼) chronometric, chronometrical.

timepiece, horological, horologiographic.

timetable, schedular.

timidity, diffident; shy.

tin, stannic, stannous.

tinamou, tinamine, tinamid; tinamiform.

tip, apical.

tissue, dissepimental; (∼ breakdown) histolytic; (∼ dweller) histozoic; (∼ eater) histophagous; (∼ production) histogenetic.

titmouse, parine.

toad, batrachian; pelobatoid; salentian; (fear of ∼s) batracophobic.

today, hodiernal.

toe, dactylic; digital; discodactylous; (absence of ∼s) adactylous; (slender ∼s) leptodactylous; (thick ∼s) pachydactylous.

toenail, ungual.

toilet, cloacal.

tolerance, (*French*) laissez-faire; xerocole.

tomb, sepulchral; tumulary.

tomboy, gamine.

tongue, glossoid; ligular, liguloid, ligulate; (*heraldry*) langued; lingual, lingulate; linguiform; (absence of ∼) aglossate; (thick ∼) pachyglossal.

tonsil, amygdaline.

tool, (bifaced ∼) acheulean; (ax shaped ∼) celtiform; Kafuan.

tooth, dental, dentoid; dentiform; odontographic; odontological; (∼ for cutting) secodont, sectorial; (∼ for shearing) carnassial; (absence of teeth) edentate, edentulate, edentulous; (broad ∼) latidentate; (fear of teeth) odontophobic; (hollow ∼) coelodont; (pain in ∼) odontalgic; (saber ∼) machairodont; (socketed ∼) gomphodont; (solid ∼) aglyphous.

toothache, odontalgic.

top, cacuminous; capital, capitate; trochiform.

topping, à la mode.

tortoise, chelonian.

tortoise shell, testudinal, testudinarious.

totality, all; universal.

tottering, shaky.

toucan, piciform.

touch, adjacent; adjoining; attingent; haptic; tactile, (*rare*) tactive; tactual (fear of ∼) aphephobic, haphephobic, haptephobic.

tow, stupeous, stupose.

tower, turrical.

town, municipal; urban.

toy, knick-knacked.

track, hippodromic; vestigal, vestigiary.

tracking, (*rare*) ichneutic.

tract, urologic.

trader, shopkeeping.

tradition, legendary, legendic; tralatitious.

tragedy, cothurnal, cothurnian.

trait, discriminating; disparate.

traitor, Iscariotic, Iscariotical; renegade; tergiversant.

trance, cataplectic; cataleptic.

tranquilizer, assuasive.

tranquillity, ataractic; disimpassioned; dispassionate, dispassioned; mild; quietsome.

transaction, negotiable; negotiatory.

transcript, apographal.

transfer, displaceable, displacive.

transference, alienable.

transformation, metastatic; versional.

transgression, peccant.

transience, ephemeral.

translation, metaphrastic, metaphrastical.

transliteration, metagraphic.

translucense, perspicuous.

transmutation, (chemical ∼) alchemic.

transparency, hyaline, hyalescent; perspicuous.

transportation, vehiculary, vehiculatory.

travel, viaggiatory; viatic; (space ∼) astronautic, austronautical.

traveler, (archaic) peregrine.

treachery, perfidious; serpentine; traitorous.

treaty, fetial, fecial.

tree, arboreal, arborean, arbored, arboreous, arborescent, arboresque, arborical; arboriform; dendriform; dendrographic, dendrographical; dendrologic, dendrological, dendrologous, dendroid; (∼ dweller) dendrophilous; (∼ eater) dendrophagous; (∼ trimming) topiarian; (worship of ∼s) dendrolatrous.

tree frog, polypedatid.

treehopper, membracid, membracine.

tree shrew, tupaiid.

trembling, palpitant; tremulant, tremulous; (fear of ∼) tremophobic.

trial and error, phobotactic.

triangle, deltoid, deltoidal. (heraldry) gyrony.

tribe, gentilic.

tribunal, Arepagitic.

triceratops, certopsid, ceratopsian.

trickery, covinous; obreptitious.

trifle, knick-knacked, knick-knacking; nugatory.

triggerfish, ballstoid, ballstid.

trilling, hirrient.

trilobite, arthropodal, arthropodan.

triteness, bathetic; hackney; platitudinal, platitudinous.

triumph, victorious.

triviality, puerile.

trouble, bothersome; pained, painful, paining.

trout, truttaceous.

Troy, Dardanian.

trumpet, buccinal.

trunk, proboscidal, proboscidate, proboscidial, proboscidean, proboscidian, proboscidiferous; proboscidiform.

trust, believable; fiduciary; reliable.

truth, alethic; alethiological; authentic; leal; sooth-fast, soothful; valid, validatory; veracious; ve-

ridical; veritable; very; (*French*)
vrai; (appearance of ∼) verisimilar, verisimilitudinous.

tuatara, sphenodont.

tube, cannular; fistular, fistulate,
fistulous; floscular; squibbish; (∼
producer) tubifacient; vasiform.

tuberculosis, cachectic, cachetical;
cachexic; consumptive; phthisic;
phthisicky.

tuft, barbate; comose; flocculate;
paniculate; scopate, scopulate;
vericulate; waddy.

tumor, bosselated; oncologic,
oncotic; sarcomatoid, sarcomatous.

tumult, boisterous; disordered.

tunic, kirtled.

tunicate, ascidiate.

tuning, modulate.

turbulence, disordered.

turf, cespititious, cespitose.

turkey, gallinaceous, galliform;
phasianid.

Turkey, Turcic.

turmoil, disordered; disruptive.

turn, fall-down; flectional; tortuous; versable; vertible.

turnip, napiform; rapaceous.

turtle, anapsid.

twelve, duodenary; duodecimal.

twenty, vicenary; vigesimal; icosian.

twig, (long ∼) vimineous.

twilight, crepuscular, crepusculine.

twin, junelle.

twist, ajoint; contorsive, contort,
contortionate, contortive; flectional, flexional; sinuous; tortuous; whelked; writhen.

twitch, saccadic; vellicative.

two, bifid; biform; binary; dimer-
ous; duadic, dual, dualistic; double; dyadic.

type, normal, normative.

typesetting, compositorial.

typhus, typhoid, typhic.

tyranny, satrapal, satrapic, satrapical.

U

ugliness, awful; grotesque; gorgonian.

ulcer, cacoethic; chancroid, chancrous; decubital; helcoid, helcological.

ultimatum, last; latemose; latest.

umbilical cord, funic.

umbilicus, omphalic.

Umbria, Iguvine.

unaccompaniment, a cappella.

uncertainty, dubitable, dubitative.

uncle, avuncular.

unconsciousness, incognizant.

uncontrollability, disobedience; disorderly.

uncourtliness, discourteous.

underhandedness, clandestine; covert; surreptitious.

underside, ventral.

understanding, discernible, discerning; empathic; noological.

understatement, meiotic.

undertaking, adventuresome.

underworld, avernal; chthonic, chthonian; Hadean; Plutonian, Plutonic; Tartarean.

undulation, fluctuable, fluctuant, fluctuous.

uneasiness, discomposed; (~ of mind) discontented; disquieted.

unemployment, jobless; leisured; otiose.

unequal sides, scalene.

unevenness, accidented; erose; jagged, jaggy.

ungraciousness, discourteous.

unhappiness, disconsolate; discontent.

union, alliable, allied; assemblable; syncretistic.

uniqueness, sui generis.

unit, (~ of weight and measure) kung; (~ of speech) syllabic.

universality, catholic; nomothetic.

universe, cosmologic, cosmological; (description of ~) cosmographic, cosmographical; (evolution of ~) cosmogonic.

unorthodoxy, (*rare*) cacodoxical, cacodoxian; heterodox.

unpredictableness, accidental.

unruliness, disobedience; disorderly.

unsophistication, simple.

unsteadiness, jiggly; titubant; waggly.

untimeliness, intempestive.
unwillingness, disinclined.
uproar, disordered.
upsilon, hypsiloid.
upward, antrorse.
urea, allophanic.
urge, (irresistible ∼) cacoethic.
urgency, importunate.
urging, adjuratory.
urination, diuretic; micturant;
  (backward ∼) retromingent;
(fear of urinating) urophobic.
urine, uretic, uric, urinous; (production of ∼) uropoictic.
urn, urceolate; urceous.
usefulness, (*rare*) proficuous.
uselessness, inutile.
uterus, hysterocystic; matrical, matricular; utricular.
utility, useful; hyerbaric; pragmatic; (lack of ∼) useless.
utterance, effable; expirate.

V

vacillation, fluctuable, fluctuant, fluctuous.

vagina, vulval, vulvar.

valiance, bold; brave; heroic.

validation, affirmable.

validity, nomic.

valor, brave.

value, no-par; precious; (~s in philosophy) axiological; (equal ~) isorropic.

valve, (absence of ~s) avalvular.

vampire bat, desmodontid.

vapor, (obsolete) fumid; nimbused.

variability, fluxional.

variation, (color ~) allochromatic.

variegation, mosaic; panached; veined, veinous, veiny.

variety, several.

varnish, laccate.

vase, urceiform.

vastness, immane.

vault, (rare) camerated; cryptal; fornicate, forniciform; tombal.

veal, vituline.

vegetation, jungly.

veil, velate.

vein, phlebographical; phleboid; vascular; venose, venous; venu-lose, venulous; (~ incision) phlebotomic, phlebotomical; (~ inflammation) phlebitic.

velum, labioguttural; labiovelar.

velvet, velutinous.

vendetta, vengeful.

vendibility, salable.

Venice, Venetian.

venom, attern, attery; veninific; virulent.

Venus, Cytherean; venerean, venerian.

Venus' flytrap, droseraceous.

verb, factitive; gerundial, gerundival, gerundive.

verdigris, (color) aeruginous, eruginous.

versatility, handy.

verse, acromonogrammatic; epithalamic; galliambic; georgic; Homeric; Iliadic; ithyphallic; lyric, lyrical; prosodic, prosodical; Sapphic; stichic; (Latin) ubi sunt; (divination using ~) stichomantic; (epic ~) bardic; (nonsense ~) amphigoric, amphigouric; (orthographic ~) acrostic.

vertebrae, urostylar.
verticality, perpendicular; upright.
vessel, conceptacular; navigerous; vascular; vasiferous, vasiform.
vexation, raggy.
vibration, fluctuable, fluctuant, fluctuous; (large ∼) sussultatory; (small ∼) succussatory.
vice, profligate.
victory, epinician; Pyrrhic.
vigilance, wakeful.
vigor, athletic; buxom; nervish, nervose, nervous; somatotonic; vascular.
vileness, evil.
villain, flagitious.
vindication, scalping.
vinegar, acetous.
vintage, vindemial.
violence, boisterous; heady; per- acute; rampacious, rampageous; unpacific; Vandemonian.
violation, sacrilegious.
violet, (color) damson.
viper, pit-headed; solenoglyphic.
virginity, vestal; zoned.
Virgin Mary, deiparous;
hyperdulic; Marist, Mariological.
viscera, abdominal; intestinal; splanchnic; somatosplanchnic.
viscosity, lentous.
viscount, viscontal.
visibility, aspectable.
vision, optic, optical; orthoptic; viewy.
vividness, eidetic.
vocabulary, lexical; phraseological.
voice, vocal, vocalic.
void, leer; vacual, vacuous.
volcano, vulcanian, vulcanean.
vole, cricetid.
volubility, fluent; fluid, fluidal.
volume, tomish.
voluptuousness, Junoesque.
vomiting, emetic; (fear of ∼) emetophobic.
voracity, cormorant; edacious.
vortex, gyratory, gyrous.
vow, votal, votary, votive.
voyage, navigant.
vulgarity, knavish; rabble; raffish; tabloid.
vulture, cathartine; raptorial.

W

wagon, plaustral.

wagtail, motacillid.

Wales, Cambrian; Cymric, Kymric; Welsh; (North ~) Venedotian.

walk, paced.

walking, ambulant, ambulatory; gressorial; pedestrian; (rare) perambulant; perambulatory; peripatetic; (heraldry) counterpassant, passant; (fear of ~) bathmophobic.

wall, circumvallate; parietal.

walnut, juglandaceous.

walrus, obenid.

wand, virgate.

wanderer, gipsyish, gypsyish; Ishmaelitish; vagabond.

wandering, circumforaneous; itinerant; nomadic; solivagant, solivagous; vagarious.

wantonness, harlot; paphian.

war, battailous; bellicose, belliferous, belligerent; martial; polemical; (after a ~) post-bellum; (before a ~) ante-bellum; (fear of ~) traumatophobic.

warmth, ardent; calid; euthermic; hearty; incalescent; thalpotic.

warning, admonitory; aposematic; monitory; sematic.

Warsaw, Varsovian.

wart, verrucose.

washing, abstergent; clysmic; detergent; lavational, lavatory.

wasp, vespal, vespine, vespoid; (digger ~) sphecid, sphecoid.

waste, macerable; recremental.

watch, chronographic, chronometric; horologic, horological.

watchfulness, alert; circumspective.

water, ad littoral; aquatic, aqueous; balneal; hydrologic, hydrological, hydrous; lentic; lotic; (~ and land) amphibiotic, amphibious; (~ cure) hydropathic; (~ - logged) uliginous; (~ vapor) atmologic, atmological; (divination using ~) hydromantic, lecanomantic, rhabdomantic; (dweller in fresh ~) hygrophilous; (dweller in stagnant ~) stagnicolous; (fear of ~) hydrophobic, hygrophobic; (fresh ~) limnetic, limnologic, limnological; (mapping of ~) hydrographic, hydrographical; (well ~ed) irriguous.

watering hole, oasal, oasean, oasitic.

water table, (above the ~) vadose.

wattle, caruncular, carunculate, carunculous.

wave, squiggly; undulant, undulate, undulatory; (full of ~s) fluctuous.

wavering, ambivalent; fluctuable, fluctuant, fluctuous; oscillatory.

wax, ceraceous, ceral, cerated; (*rare*) cereous; ceriferous, cerophilous, ceroplastic; (divination using ~) ceromantic; (engraving on ~) cerographic.

weakness, asthenic; flaccid; (*rare*) labefact; languent, languescent, languid, languishing; namby-pamby; phthisic; shilpit.

wealth, affluent; aristocratic; chrematistic; opulent; plutological; (craving for ~) plutomanic; (fear of ~) chrematophobic.

weaponry, armed.

wear, used.

weasel, arctoidean; mustelid, musteline.

weather, climatological.

weathercock, vaned.

web, anisopogonous; arachnoid, arachnoidal; araneous; retiary, reticulate; retiform.

wedge, cuneal, cuneate, cuneiform; sphenic, sphenoid.

week, hebdomadal.

weeping, begrutten.

weevil, curculionid.

weight, grievous; heavy; moliminous; ponderal, ponderous.

welcome, salutatory.

well, phratic.

werewolf, lycanthropic.

west, Hesperian; Occidental; occasive; ponent.

wetness, aquose; madid.

whale, cetacean, cetaceous, cetic; cetological; (right ~) balaenid; (sperm ~) physeterid, physeteroid. See also *rorqual*.

wheal, urticate.

wheat, caryopsid; frumentaceous.

wheat rust, puccinoid.

wheel, rotal; rotiform; trochal.

whelk, buccinid.

Whig Club, Kit-cat.

whimsy, facical; fanciful, fancy.

whinny, hinnible.

whip, flagellant, flagelliform.

whirlpool, vortical.

whiskers, bearded, beardy; vibrissal.

white cell deficiency, leucopenic, leukopenic.

whiteness, alabaster, alabastrine; blenching; candent; etiolated; hoary; niveous.

whooping cough, pertussal.

whorl, verticillate.

wick, snuffy.

wickedness, bad, baddish; caitiff; (*archaic*) facinorous; fiendish; fierce; flagitious; heinous; Jezebelian, Jezebelish; nefarious, villainous.

widow, discovert; vidual, viduate.

width, ampliate; broad; (lack of ~) narrow.

wife, uxorial; (killing of ~) uxoricidal.

wildness, ramage.
will, heady; volent; voluntary; (*legal*) testamentary.
Winchester College, Wykehamist, Wykehamical.
wind, Aeolian; anemological; (*rare*) vental; (dread of ∼) anemophobic; (love of ∼) anemophilic, anemophilous; (measurement of ∼) anemographic.
window, fenestral.
windpipe, tracheal, tracheate.
wine, oenological; palateful; vinaceous, vinic, viniferous, vinous; viticultural; (∼ making) oenopoetic; (divination using ∼) oenomantic, enomantic, oinomantic; (hatred of ∼) oenophobic, enophobic, oinophobic; (love of ∼) oenophilic, enophilic, oinophilic.
wing, alate; aliferous, aliform; pterygoid; (*heraldry*) displayed, segreant; (absence of ∼) exalate; (broad ∼) latipennate; (four ∼s) tetrapterous; (large ∼) macropterous; (transparent ∼) hyalopterous; (two ∼s) bialate, dipterous; (under ∼) subalary, subalate.
wink, nictitant; palpebral.
winter, Boreal; brumal; hibernal; hiemal.
wisdom, Apollonian; Minervan; sage; sapient, sapiential, Solonian, Solonic.
wish, optative; precatory.
wit, Falstaffian; lepid; waggish.
witchcraft, sortilegic, sortilegious.
withdrawal, abient.
withering, marcid.
witness, compurgatory.

wizard, druidic, druidical; necromantic.
wolf, lupine; lycanthropic; thooid.
wolverine, mustelid.
woman, feminine, feministic; gynecic, gynecian, gynecoid, gynic; (*rare*) muliebral, muliebrile; (fear of women) gynephobic, gynophobic; (government by women) gynarchic, gyneocratic; (hatred of women) misogynic, misogynous, misogynistic; (love of women) philogynous, (*rare*) mulierose; (killing of women) femicidal; (resembling an old ∼) anicular.
womb, matrical, matricular; uterine.
wombat, vombatid.
wonder, mirific.
wood, lathen; ligenous; lignescent, ligniform; nemoral; xylary, xyloid; (eating ∼) hylophagous, xylophagous.
woodcock, charadrine, charadrioid; scolopacine.
woodpecker, picine, piciform.
woods, sylvan; sylvatic.
wool, floccose, flocculent; lanate, lanated, lanose; noily; pashmina; ulotrichous.
word, holophrastic; lexical; monepic; philologic, philological; (∼ blindness) dyslexic; (∼ dispute) logomachic, logomachical; (∼ formation) rhematic; (∼ meaning) lexicologic, lexicological, semantic, semasiological, semeiologic, semeiological; (derivation of ∼s) etymologic, etymological; (divination using ∼s) logomantic; (equivocal ∼s)

parisological; (long ∼) sesquipe-
dalian; (misuse of ∼s) catachrestic, catachrestical; (new ∼) neol-
ogistic, neologistical; (offensive
∼s) dyphemistic; (opposing ∼s)
antiphrastic, antiphrastical; (polite
∼s) euphemistic; (redundant
∼s) pleonastic; (scornful ∼s)
deristic; (technical ∼s) orismologic, orismological; (worship of
∼s) grammatolatrous, logolatrous.

wordiness, logorrheic; prolix; verbose; voluble.

work, industrious; operose; (fear of
∼) ergasiophobic; (hatred of ∼)
ergophobic; (love of ∼) ergophilic.

workroom, laboratorial, labora-
torian.

world, mondial.

worm, helminthic; larval; nemer-
toid; scolecoid; vermian,
vermicious, vermicular, vermiculated, vermiculose, vermiform,
verminal; (fear of ∼s) helminthophobic, scoleciphobic, vermiphobic.

worrisome, carking.

worship, adoring; idolatrous; liturgical; (∼ of humans) anthropo-
latrous; (∼ of phallus) ithyphallic.

worth, (absence of ∼) baff; (lack
of ∼) disingenuous, gimcrack;
valuable.

wound, discoid; scarry; vulnerable,
vulnerary.

wrath, achilean.

wreath, (*heraldry*) tortillé.

wrestling, palaestral, palestral.

wriggle, scriggly.

wrinkle, (*archaic*) corrugate; riggy;
rugose, rugous.

wrist, carpal.

writer, auctorial; journalistic.

writing, cursive; graphic, graphologic; ideographic, ideographical;
literal; scribblative, scribblatory,
scribbled; scriptitory, scriptorial,
scriptory; scriptural; (bad ∼)
cacographic; (dislike of ∼)
graphophobic; (good ∼) orthographic.

X

X, (∼ shape) decussate.
x ray, fluoroscopic; pyelographic; radiographic, radiographical; radiologic, radiological.

Y

Y, (∼ shape) hypsiliform, hypsiloid; ypsiliform.

yak, poephagous.

yam, dioscorine.

yawn, oscitant.

year, per annum; (one ∼) annual; (two ∼s) biennial; (three ∼s) triennial; (four ∼s) quadrennial; (five ∼s) quinquennial; (six ∼s) sexennial; (seven ∼s) septennial, septenary; (eight ∼s) octennial; (nine ∼s) novennial; (ten ∼s) decennial, decennary; (fifteen ∼s) quindecennial; (twenty ∼s) vicennial, vigentennial, vigintennial; (fifty ∼s) semicentennial, semicentenary; (one hundred ∼s) centennial, centenary; (one hundred fifty ∼s) sesquicentennial; (two hundred ∼s) bicentennial, bicentenary; (three hundred ∼s) tercentenary, tricentennial; (four hundred ∼s) quadricentennial; (five hundred ∼s) quinquecentennial; (one thousand ∼s) millennial.

yellow fruit, chrysocarpous.

yellowing, jaundiced.

yellowish green, chlorogenic.

yellow jacket, (insect) vespid, vespine, vespoid.

yellowness, croceous; flavid; gamboge; icterine, ictritious, icteroid; saffron, saffrony; vitelline; xanthic, xanthous; (canary ∼) capucine; (straw ∼) festucine; (quince ∼) meline.

yesterday, hesternal.

yolk, lecithic, lecithal; vitelline; (absence of ∼) alecithal; (small ∼) microlecithal.

young, (many ∼) polytocous.

youth, adolescent; junior; juvenal, juvenile; kid; (regaining ∼) juvenescent.

Z

zeal, fanatic, fanatical.
zebra, hippotigrine.

Zeus, Panomphaean, Panomphaic.
Zwinglian, sacramentarian.

A

accessory, **contribution**
accidental, **unpredictableness**
accidented, **unevenness**
accipitral, **goshawk, hawk**
accipitrid, **eagle, goshawk**
accipitrine, **goshawk, hawk**
acclivitous, **inclination, slope**
acclivous, **rise**
accolent, **neighbor**
accollé, **collar, joining**
accommodable, **adaptation**
accommodating, **help**
accommodative, **adaptation**
accomplished, **completeness, estab-**
  lishment
accordant, **agreement**
according, **agreement**
accostable, **access**
accosted, **support**
accountable, **answer, explanation**
accredited, **recognition**
accrescent, **growth**
accretionary, **growth**
accretive, **growth**
acculturational, **borrowing**
accumbent, **reclination**
accumulable, **collection**
accumulate, **collection**
accumulative, **collection**
accurate, **precision**
accusational, **charge**
accusative, **object**
accusatory, **charge**
accusive, **charge**
accustomed, **habit**
acephalic, **brain, decapitation, head**
acephalous, **brain, decapitation, head**
acerb, **acid, anger, sourness**
acerbate, **irritation**
acerb Draconic, **severity**
acerbic, **acid, sourness**
acerous, **antennae, horn, tentacle**
acervate, **growth**
acervative, **heap**
acervuline, **accumulation, heap, pile**
acesodyne, **relief**
acetabular, **cup**
acetarious, **salad**
acetic, **acid, sourness**

acetonic, **liquid**
acetose, **acid, sourness**
acetous, **sourness, vinegar**
Achaean, **Greece**
Achaemenian, **Persian**
acheronian, **darkness**
acherontic, **darkness**
acheulean, **tool**
achievable, **accomplishment**
achilean, **wrath**
Achillean, **strength**
acholic, **bile, deficiency**
achromatic, **color, refraction**
acicular, **needle**
aciculate, **needle**
acid, **sourness**
acidoprotelyctic, **digestion**
acidulous, **causticity**
acidy, **tartness**
acinaciform, **scimitar**
aciniform, **grape**
acinotubular, **gland**
acipenserid, **sturgeon**
acipenserine, **sturgeon**
acknowledgeable, **recognition**
acknowledged, **recognition**
aclinal, **flatness**
acock, **tilt**
acomous, **baldness**
acoumetric, **hearing**
acousticolateral, **ear**
acousticophobic, **fear, noise**
acquiescent, **submission**
acquired, **gain, possession**
acquisite, **gain, possession**
acquisitive, **possession**
acranial, **head**
acrid, **sharpness**
acridian, **grasshopper**
acridid, **grasshopper**
acrimonious, **anger, bitterness, mal-**
  ice, severity
acritochromatic, **blindness, color**
acrobatic, **gymnastics**
acrocranial, **head**
acrogenous, **growth**
acrographic, **engraving**
acrographical, **engraving**
acrolithic, **cover**

admissive, **allowability**
admitted, **acknowledgment**
admonitory, **warning**
adnominal, **modifier**
adolescent, **youth**
adoptable, **taking**
adoring, **worship**
adorned, **decoration**
ad rem, **relevance**
adroit, **dexterity, shrewdness**
adscititious, **supplement**
adscititious;adventitious, **addition**
adscript, **attachment**
adscripted, **attachment**
adscriptitious, **attachment**
adscriptive, **attachment**
adulatory, **praise**
adult, **maturation**
adulterant, **corruption, debasement, falseness**
adulterate, **corruption, debasement, falseness**
adulterine, **corruption**
adulterous, **infidelity**
adumbral, **shade, shadow**
adumbrant, **shadow**
adumbrative, **foreshadowing, prediction, shadow**
ad valorem, **tax**
advantageous, **favor**
adventive, **immigrant**
adventuresome, **danger, undertaking**
adventurous, **danger**
adverbal, **modifier**
adverbial, **modifier**
adversary, **antagonist**
adverse, **disinclination, reluctance**
advertent, **attention**
advertisable, **information**
adviceful, **attention**
advised, **reflection**
advocatory, **defender**
aedeagal, **phallus**
aedicular, **niche**
aedine, **mosquito**
aedistic, **language**
aelurophobic, **cat, fear**
Aeolian, **wind**
aeolid, **nudibranch**

aeonian, **eternity**
aeonic, **lasting**
aerial, **atmosphere**
aeriform, **air**
aerobatic, **stunt**
aerodonetic, **glide**
aerodromic, **flying**
aerodynamic, **flying**
aerohydrous, **container**
aerolithological, **meteorite**
aerolitic, **meteorite**
aerologic, **air, atmosphere**
aerological, **air, atmosphere, meteorology**
aeromantic, **air, atmosphere**
aeromarine, **navigation**
aerometric, **air, measurement**
aeronautic, **balloon**
aeronautical, **flight**
aerophilatelic, **collecting**
aerophobic, **air, fear**
aerophonic, **instrument**
aerostatic, **balloon**
aerotechnical, **flight**
aeruginous, **verdigris**
aeschynomenous, **sensitivity**
Aesculapian, **healing, medicine**
Aesopian, **dissemblance, fable**
Aesopic, **fable**
aesthetic, **beauty**
aethereal, **heavens**
affable, **ease, pleasance**
affectable, **influence**
affected, **pretention**
affectional, **emotion, feeling**
affectionate, **emotion, feeling**
affectionated, **emotion, feeling**
affective, **emotion**
affectuous, **emotion**
afferent, **conveyance**
affinal, **marriage**
affined, **connection**
affinitive, **relationship**
affirmable, **validation**
affirmative, **ratification**
affirmatory, **ratification**
afflated, **inspiration**
afflicted, **affectation**
afflictive, **cause**

amical, **friend**
amicidal, **friend, killing**
ammophilous, **sand**
amnesic, **memory**
amorphic, **form**
amorphous, **form**
amphibiotic, **land, water**
amphibious, **land, water**
amphibological, **language**
amphibolous, **language**
amphidesmous, **ligament**
amphierotic, **sex**
amphigonic, **reproduction**
amphigoric, **verse**
amphigouric, **verse**
ampliate, **enlargement, width**
ampullaceous, **flask**
ampullate, **flask**
ampulliform, **dilation, flask**
amygdalaceous, **peach, plum**
amygdaline, **tonsil**
amyliferous, **starch**
anacamptic, **reflection**
anacanthous, **sole**
anacardic, **cashew**
anacathartic, **emetic**
anachronistic, **chronology**
anachronistical, **chronology**
anachronous, **chronology**
anaclastic, **refraction**
anaclitic, **dependency**
Anacreontic, **gaiety, lyric**
anacusic, **deafness**
anaglyphic, **carving, embossment,
 relief**
anagogic, **allegory, mystic**
analectic, **selection**
analgesic, **pain**
analgetic, **pain**
analogical, **relation, similarity**
analphabetic, **illiteracy**
analytic, **clarification, logic, reason,
 separation**
anamorphous, **distortion**
anapestic, **foot**
anapsid, **turtle**
anarchic, **government**
anasarcous, **dropsy, edema**
anastatic, **convalescence**

anchoretic, **monk**
anchoritic, **monk, recluse**
anchylotic, **stiffness**
ancient, **antiquity**
ancipital, **edge**
anconoid, **elbow**
ancylotic, **stiffness**
Andean, **Andes**
Andine, **Andes**
andric, **man**
androgynous, **sex**
androphagous, **cannibalism**
androphobic, **fear, man**
anemographic, **wind**
anemological, **wind**
anemophilic, **wind**
anemophilous, **wind**
anemophobic, **fear, wind**
angiographic, **blood**
angiographical, **blood**
angioid, **blood vessel**
angiological, **blood vessel**
angiopathological, **blood vessel**
Anglican, **England**
Anglophilic, **England**
Anglophobic, **England, fear**
anguiform, **snake**
anguilliform, **eel**
angulous, **corner**
angustirostrate, **snout**
aniconic, **icon, idol, symbol**
anicular, **woman**
anidian, **form**
anile, **flightiness**
anisodynamous, **growth**
anisogamous, **conjugation**
anisopogonous, **web**
ankylotic, **stiffness**
annotinous, **one year**
annual, **year**
annular, **ring**
anodyne, **relief**
anopheline, **mosquito**
anorectic, **appetite**
anorectous, **appetite**
anorexic, **appetite**
anseriform, **duck**
anserine, **goose, stupidity**
antarchistic, **government**

atrabilious, **behavior, temper**
atrichic, **baldness**
atropid, **book louse**
attent, **heed**
attentional, **heed**
attentive, **heed**
attenuate, **thinness**
attern, **venom**
attery, **poison, venom**
Attic, **Greece, humor**
attid, **spider**
attingent, **contact, touch**
auburn, **redness**
au courant, **fashion**
auctionary, **sale**
auctorial, **author, writer**
audient, **attention, listening**
auditive, **assembly, audience**
auditory, **assembly, audience**
auditual, **audience, assembly**
augural, **omen**
augurous, **omen**
aulic, **language**
aural, **ear, hearing**
aurantiaceous, **orange**
aureate, **gold**
auric, **ear**
auricular, **ear, hearing**
auriferous, **gold**
aurific, **gold**
aurinasal, **ear**
aurophobic, **dislike, gold**
auroral, **dawn, radiance**
aurorean, **dawn**
aurous, **ear, gold**
auscultatory, **listening**
austere, **bitterness, sternness**
austral, **south**
austronautical, **travel**
autarchic, **sovereignty**
autarchical, **sovereignty**
autarkic, **self**
autarkical, **self**
authentic, **truth, credibility**
autocephalous, **self**
autochthonous, **indigenousness**
autocratic, **sovereignty**
autocthonous, **native**
autogamic, **self**
autogenous, **self**

autognostic, **self**
autolatrous, **self**
autological, **self**
autolytic, **degeneration, self**
automatic, **action**
autonomous, **government, independence**
autophilic, **narcissism, self**
autophobic, **fear, self**
autopotamic, **stream**
autotelic, **end, purpose**
autumnal, **fall**
auxetic, **growth**
available, **assistance, beneficiality**
avalvular, **valve**
avaricious, **greed**
avascular, **blood vessel**
average, **normality**
avernal, **underworld**
avian, **bird**
avicolous, **bird**
avuncular, **pawnbroker, uncle**
awful, **ugliness**
axenic, **sterility**
axial, **axis**
axillant, **armpit, shoulder**
axillar, **armpit, shoulder**
axillary, **armpit, shoulder**
axiological, **ethics, value**
azonic, **localness**
azure, **blueness**
azymous, **leavening**

B

babblative, **chatter, loquacity, talk**
babblesome, **chatter, loquacity, talk**
babbling, **chatter, loquacity, talk**
babyish, **infant**
baccaceous, **berry**
baccate, **berry, pulp**
bacchanal, **orgy**
bacchanalian, **inebriation, intoxication, revel, drunkenness, orgy**

Index

burlesque, **mockery**
bursal, **revenue**
bursiform, **pouch**
bushy, **shrub, thicket**
busy, **engagement, occupation**
butyraceous, **butter, lard**
buxom, **compliancy, health, obedience, vigor**
byssiferous, **silk**
byssine, **silk**
byssoid, **cotton, silk**

C

cabalic, **mystery**
cabalistic, **mystery**
cabalistical, **mystery**
caballine, **horse**
Cabirean, **metalworker**
Cabirian, **metalworker**
Cabiric, **metalworker**
Cabiritic, **metalworker**
cachaemic, **blood**
cachectic, **cancer, tuberculosis**
cachectical, **cancer**
cachemic, **blood**
cachetical, **tuberculosis**
cachexic, **cancer, tuberculosis**
cachinnatory, **laughter**
cacodemoniac, **demon, devil,
nightmare**
cacodemonial, **devil, nightmare**
cacodemonic, **demon, nightmare**
cacodoxian, **unorthodoxy**
cacodoxical, **unorthodoxy**
cacoethic, **mania, ulcer, urge**
cacogastric, **dyspepsia**
cacogenic, **degeneration**
cacographic, **penmanship, spelling,
writing**
cacographical, **penmanship, spelling**
cacograstric, **digestion**
cacological, **diction, pronunciation**
caconymic, **name**
cacophonic, **discordance, dissonance,
noise, sound**

cacophonical, **discordance**
cacophonous, **discordance, dissonance, noise, sound**
cacoëpistic, **pronunciation**
cacozealous, **imitation**
cacuminous, **top**
cadastral, **boundary, land**
cadaveric, **corpse**
cadaverous, **corpse**
cade, **pet**
cadenced, **rhythm**
cadent, **descent**
caducicorn, **antler**
caducous, **lapse**
caecodemoniac, **demon**
caecodemonic, **demon, devil**
caesural, **interruption**
caesuric, **break**
cainophobic, **fear, novelty**
cainotophobic, **novelty**
caitiff, **coward, meanness, wickedness**
calamiferous, **reed**
calamiform, **reed**
calcaneal, **heel**
calcanean, **heel**
calcareous, **lime**
calced, **shoe**
calceiform, **slipper**
calcinatory, **disintegration**
calcitrant, **stubbornness**
calcographic, **chalk**
calcographical, **chalk**
calculiform, **pebble**
calculous, **gravel**
Caledonian, **Scotland**
calefacient, **heat**
calentural, **ardor, fever, passion**
calescent, **heat**
caliciform, **bell**
calid, **burning, warmth**
caliginous, **darkness, obscurity**
caliological, **bird, nest**
calisthenic, **exercise, gymnastics**
callid, **shrewdness**
calligraphic, **penmanship, handwriting**
calligraphical, **handwriting, penmanship**

capsulogenous, **case**
captious, **criticism, faultfinding**
capucine, **yellowness**
carangid, **amberfish, pompano**
carangoid, **amberfish, pompano**
carapacic, **shell**
caravanserial, **hotel, inn**
carboniferous, **coal**
carbonigerous, **coal**
carbonous, **charcoal**
carcharinid, **shark**
carcharodont, **shark**
Cardanic, **gimbals**
cardiac, **heart, stomach**
cardiacal, **heart, stomach**
cardiacean, **cockles**
cardial, **heart**
cardiform, **rasp, scraper**
cardinal, **hinge**
cardinalic, **cardinal**
cardiod, **heart**
cardiologic, **heart**
cardiological, **heart**
cardiopathic, **heart**
cardiophobic, **fear, heart**
cardophagous, **donkey**
carduaceous, **aster, thistle**
cardueline, **goldfinch**
caricaceous, **papaya**
caridean, **shrimp**
caridoid, **shrimp**
carinal, **keel**
carinate, **keel, ridge**
carinated, **keel**
cariniform, **keel**
carious, **cavity, decay**
caritative, **charity**
carking, **worrisome**
carlish, **churl, coarseness, rudeness**
Carlovingian, **Charles**
carminative, **flatulence**
carmine, **redness**
carnal, **bloodthirstiness, flesh, sex**
carnassial, **tooth**
Carneian, **Apollo**
carneous, **flesh**
carnic, **flesh**
carniferous, **flesh**
carnificial, **butcher, executioner**

carniform, **flesh**
carnivorous, **animal, flesh, meat**
carnose, **flesh**
carnous, **flesh**
Caroline, **Charles**
Carolingian, **Charles**
Carolinian, **Charles**
carotic, **stupor**
carpal, **wrist**
carpogenic, **fruit**
carpogenous, **fruit**
carpological, **fruit**
carpophagous, **eating, fruit**
Cartesian, **Descartes**
Carthusian, **Charterhouse School, Chartreuse**
cartilagineous, **gristle**
cartilaginous, **gristle**
cartographic, **chart, map**
cartographical, **chart, map**
carucal, **plow, plowland**
carucated, **plow, plowland**
caruncular, **growth, wattle**
carunculate, **wattle**
carunculated, **knot**
carunculous, **growth, wattle**
caryopsid, **barley, wheat**
caseous, **cheese**
cassideous, **helmet**
Castalian, **Muses**
castellar, **castle**
castellate, **castle**
castellated, **battlement**
castigable, **punishment**
castorial, **hat**
castral, **camp**
castrensian, **camp**
casuistic, **case history**
catachrestic, **word**
catachrestical, **word**
cataclysmic, **disruption**
catacoustic, **echo**
catacumbal, **catacomb**
catadioptric, **reflection, refraction**
catagenetic, **evolution**
Cataian, **Cathay**
catalactic, **exchange**
Catalan, **Catalonia**
cataleptic, **immobility, trance**

ceratorhine, **rhinoceros**
ceraunomantic, **thunder**
ceraunophobic, **fear, lightning, thunder**
Cerberean, **custodian, guardian**
Cerberic, **custodian, guardian**
cercal, **tail**
cereal, **grain**
cerealian, **grain**
cerealic, **grain**
cerebral, **brain**
cerebrational, **brain**
cerebric, **brain**
cerebriform, **brain, convolution**
cerebroid, **brain**
ceremonialistic, **ritual**
cereous, **wax**
ceriferous, **wax**
cernuous, **drooping**
cerographic, **engraving, wax**
ceromantic, **wax**
cerophilous, **wax**
ceroplastic, **wax**
certopsid, **triceratops**
cerulean, **blueness**
ceruleous, **blueness**
cerulescent, **blueness**
cerumiferous, **earwax**
ceruminiparous, **earwax**
ceruminous, **earwax**
cervical, **neck**
cervicorn, **antler**
cervid, **deer, elk, moose**
cervine, **deer, elk, moose**
cesious, **bluish gray**
cespititious, **turf**
cespitose, **turf**
cestodan, **tapeworm**
cestoid, **tapeworm**
Cestrian, **Cheshire, Chester**
cetacean, **dolphin, porpoise, whale**
cetaceous, **dolphin, porpoise, whale**
cetic, **whale**
cetological, **whale**
chaetiferous, **bristle**
chaetophorous, **bristle**
chaetotactic, **bristle**
chalastic, **laxative**
chalcographic, **copper, drawing**

chalcolithic, **copper**
chalcomantic, **brass**
Chaldean, **astrology, magic, occult**
chalybeous, **blueness, bluish black**
chamaeprosopic, **face**
chamecephalic, **skull**
chamecephalous, **skull**
chancroid, **ulcer**
chancrous, **ulcer**
chapitral, **chapter**
characterologic, **personality**
characterological, **personality**
charadriiform, **auk, guillemot, gull, murre, puffin**
charadrine, **plover, sandpiper, snipe, woodcock**
charadrioid, **plover, sandpiper, snipe, woodcock**
charlatanic, **behavior**
charnel, **burial**
chartaceous, **paper**
chauvinistic, **nationalism, patriot**
cheirographic, **handwriting**
cheirographical, **handwriting**
cheiromantic, **palmistry**
cheironomic, **gesture**
chelate, **claw**
cheliferous, **claw**
cheliform, **claw**
chelonian, **tortoise**
chelydroid, **snapping turtle**
cherophobic, **fear, happiness**
cherubic, **angel**
cherubical, **angel**
chevaline, **horse**
chiasmal, **cross, fusion**
chiasmatic, **fusion**
chiasmic, **cross, intersection**
chiastic, **intersection**
chiliadal, **millennium, thousand**
chiliadic, **millennium, thousand**
chiliastic, **millenarian**
chionableptic, **snow**
chionablepical, **blindness**
chiral, **hand**
chirocosmetic, **hand**
chirognomic, **hand**
chirographic, **handwriting, penmanship**

cuneate, **wedge**
cuneiform, **wedge**
cunicular, **burrow, mine**
cupreous, **copper**
cupric, **copper**
cuprous, **copper**
cupuliferous, **beech tree, birch tree, catkin, oak**
curative, **remedy**
curculionid, **weevil**
cucurbitaceous, **pumpkin**
curial, **court**
curricular, **carriage, course**
cursive, **course, running, writing**
cursorial, **running**
curtal, **brevity**
curtate, **brevity**
curule, **dignity**
curvant, **bend**
curvate, **bend**
cuspal, **point**
cuspate, **apex, point**
cuspid, **point**
cuspidal, **apex, point**
cuspidate, **apex, point**
custodial, **guardian**
cutaneal, **skin**
cutaneous, **skin**
cuterebrid, **botfly**
cuticular, **skin**
cutigerous, **skin**
cyanean, **blueness**
cyaneous, **blueness**
cyanic, **blueness**
cyathiform, **cup**
cyclarthroidal, **pivot**
cycloid, **circle**
cycloidal, **circle**
Cyclopean, **giant, hugeness, massiveness**
Cyclopic, **giant, massiveness**
cyclopteroid, **lumpfish**
cyclopterous, **lumpfish**
cyclorrhaphous, **housefly**
cyclostomate, **hagfish, lamprey**
cyclostomatous, **hagfish, lamprey**
cyclostome, **hagfish, lamprey**
cyclothymic, **manic depression**
cygnine, **swan**
Cyllenian, **commerce, lying, thievery**

cymbate, **boat**
cymbiform, **boat**
cymophanous, **chatoyancy, opalescence**
Cymric, **Wales**
cynaraceous, **artichoke, thistle**
cynareous, **artichoke**
cynaroid, **artichoke, thistle**
cynegetic, **hunting**
cynic, **dog, Dog Star, Sirius**
cynipid, **gallfly**
cynipidous, **gallfly**
cynipoid, **gallfly**
cynocephalic, **dog**
cynocephalous, **dog**
cynoid, **dog**
cynophobic, **dog, fear, pseudorabies**
cynosural, **guide**
cyphellate, **cup**
cypraeid, **cowrie**
cypraeiform, **cowrie**
cypraeoid, **cowrie**
cypridophobic, **fear, sex**
cyprine, **cypress**
cyprinid, **bream, carp, goldfish, minnow, shiner**
cyprinoid, **bream, carp, goldfish, minnow, shiner**
Cyrillic, **alphabet**
Cytherean, **Aphrodite, Venus**
cytodieretic, **cell**
cytoid, **cell**
cytologic, **cell**
cytological, **cell**
cytophagous, **cell**

D

dactylar, **digit**
dactylic, **digit, foot, toe**
dactyliographic, **engraving, ring**
dactyliologic, **ring**
dactyliomantic, **ring**
dactylographic, **fingerprint**

disjointed, **dislocation, incoherency**
disjunct, **incontiguousness**
disjunctional, **incontiguousness**
disjunctive, **parting**
disleal, **disloyalty, perfidy**
dismal, **dejection, depression, discouragement, dreariness, luck**
dismissive, **denial, rebuffing, refusal, renouncement, repudiation**
dismissory, **dismissal**
Disneyesque, **animation**
disobedience, **insubordination, uncontrollability, unruliness**
disomic, **duplication**
disordered, **commotion, tumult, turbulence, turmoil, uproar**
disorderly, **insubordination, uncontrollability, unruliness**
disordinate, **exorbitance, extravagance, extremity, immoderation, intemperance**
disorganized, **incoherency**
disoriented, **dislocation, displacement, misplacement**
disparate, **trait**
dispassionate, **calmness, composure, coolness, equanimity, tranquillity**
dispassioned, **calmness, composure, coolness, equanimity, tranquillity**
dispatchful, **accomplishment, achievement, realization**
dispendious, **extravagance**
dispensable, **remittance**
dispensative, **administration**
dispermous, **seed**
disperse, **apportionment**
dispirited, **darkness, dejection, depression, melancholy, sadness**
dispiriting, **cheer**
dispiteous, **atrocity, brutality, cruelty, harshness, inhumanity**
displaceable, **replacement, transfer**
displacive, **removal, replacement, transfer**
displayed, **wing**
disponible, **arrangement**
disposed, **constitution, temperament**
dispositive, **inclination**
dispossessed, **deprivation**

disprovable, **confutation, refutation**
disputable, **contestation**
disputant, **altercation, contention, controversy**
disputatious, **argument, contestation**
disquieted, **uneasiness**
disquisative, **examination**
disquisitional, **examination**
disquisitive, **inquiry, investigation**
disquisitorial, **examination**
disquisitory, **examination**
disregardful, **neglect, omission**
disrespectful, **action**
disruptive, **turmoil**
disruptured, **split**
dissatisfied, **discontent, displeasure**
dissectional, **division**
dissective, **division**
dissentaneous, **discord**
dissentient, **disagreement**
dissentious, **disagreement**
dissepimental, **tissue**
dissertational, **discussion**
dissertative, **discussion**
disserviceable, **damage, harm, injury**
dissident, **disagreement**
dissimilative, **comparison, contrast**
dissimilatory, **comparison, contrast, difference**
dissimulative, **difference, dissemblance**
dissolute, **revel**
distaff, **female**
distal, **remoteness**
distant, **remoteness**
disyllabic, **syllable**
dithyrambic, **eloquence**
diuretic, **urination**
diurnal, **day**
divaricate, **fork**
divulgatory, **publicity**
divulsive, **separation**
dodecagonal, **side**
dolabriform, **ax, cleaver**
dolichocephalic, **head**
dolichocephalous, **head**
dolichocerous, **antennae**
dolichocranic, **skull**
dolichofacial, **face**

dolichoid, **narrowness**
dolichopodous, **foot**
dolioform, **barre**
dolmenic, **menhir, monolith**
doloriferous, **grief, anguish, pain**
dolorific, **anguish, grief, pain**
dolorous, **anguish, grief, pain**
domal, **house**
domanial, **manor**
domestic, **country, family, household, nation**
domiciliary, **dwelling, residence**
dominical, **Jesus Christ, Sunday**
donaciform, **mollusk**
doré, **gold**
dormant, **latency, sleep**
dormient, **latency, sleep**
dorsal, **back, posterior**
dorsicollar, **back**
dorsiferous, **back**
dorsispinal, **back**
dorsolateral, **back**
doryline, **ant**
double, **two**
dour, **gloom**
doxastic, **belief**
doxological, **praise**
Draconian, **law, severity**
draconic, **dragon, month**
dramaturgic, **acting**
dramaturgical, **acting**
dreamy, **reverie**
droitural, **ownership**
dromic, **racecourse**
droseraceous, **Venus' flytrap, sundew**
drosophilid, **fly**
droughty, **dryness, rain**
drouthy, **dryness, rain**
druidic, **wizard**
druidical, **wizard**
drupaceous, **cherry, peach, plum**
dryadic, **nymph**
duadic, **two**
dual, **two**
dualistic, **two**
dubious, **doubt, hesitation**
dubitable, **uncertainty**
dubitative, **uncertainty**
ducal, **duke**
dulocratic, **government, slave**

dulotic, **enslavement**
dumose, **bush**
dumous, **bush**
duodecimal, **twelve**
duodenary, **twelve**
duplicatus, **cloud**
duteous, **obedience**
dutiful, **obedience**
dyadic, **two**
dynastic, **ruler**
dynastical, **ruler**
dyphemistic, **word**
dysarthric, **stuttering**
dyschromatopic, **blindness**
dyscrasic, **health**
dyscratic, **health**
dysgenic, **deterioration**
dyslexic, **word**
dyslogistic, **censure, disapproval**
dysmorphophobic, **fear, fear, monster**
dyspeptic, **digestion, indigestion**
dysphagic, **swallowing**
dysphoric, **discomfort**
dystocial, **birth**

E

eager, **anxiousness, avidness, desire**
ear-leaved, **lobe**
early, **beginning**
earnest, **seriousness, sincerity, solemnity**
earthy, **soil**
easy, **facility, freedom**
eatable, **consuming, devouring**
ebb, **depth**
ebon, **blackness, darkness**
ebony, **darkness**
ebullient, **agitation, boiling, effervescence, enthusiasm**
ebullitive, **boiling, effervescence**
eburnated, **ivory**
eburnean, **ivory**

eburneoid, **ivory**
eburneous, **ivory**
ecaudate, **tail**
ecbatic, **consequence, result**
eccentric, **deviation, strangeness**
eccentrical, **deviation, strangeness**
ecchymotic, **bruise**
ecclesial, **church, government**
ecclesiastic, **church, clergy, government**
ecclesiastical, **church, clergy, government**
ecclesioclastic, **church**
ecclesiographic, **church**
ecclesiographical, **church**
ecclesiolatrous, **church**
ecclesiologic, **church**
ecclesiological, **church**
ecclesiophobic, **church**
eccritic, **excretion**
ecdysial, **shedding**
echinal, **sea urchin**
echinate, **bristle, prickle, spine**
echinital, **sea urchin**
echinoderm, **sea urchin**
echinodermatous, **sea urchin**
echinodermic, **sea urchin**
echinoid, **sea urchin**
echinulate, **prickle, spine**
echinuliform, **prickle, spine**
echoic, **imitation**
echolalic, **imitation**
eclectic, **selection**
eclectical, **selection**
ecliptic, **circle**
ecliptical, **circle**
ecological, **environment**
economic, **management**
ecophobic, **fear, home**
ecstatic, **joy, rapture**
ectal, **exterior**
ectomorphic, **body, thinness**
ectopic, **location**
ecumenic, **church**
ecumenical, **church**
edacious, **appetite, eating, feeding, voracity**
edaphic, **soil**
edematous, **swelling**

Edenic, **paradise**
edentate, **aardvark, armadillo, sloth, tooth**
edentulate, **tooth**
edentulous, **tooth**
edible, **consuming, devouring**
edictal, **decree, notice**
edificable, **building, construction, structure**
edifical, **building**
edificatory, **building, construction, structure**
edificial, **construction, structure**
editorial, **publisher**
educable, **cultivation, development, teaching**
educatable, **cultivation, development, teaching**
educated, **instruction, intelligence**
educative, **instruction**
eerie, **gloom**
effable, **utterance**
effaceable, **disappearance, erasure, obliteration**
effectful, **fulfillment**
effectible, **fulfillment, realization**
effective, **fulfillment, production, realization**
effectual, **fulfillment, production, realization**
effeminate, **female**
efferent, **discharge**
effervescent, **bubble**
effervescive, **bubble**
efflorescent, **blooming, flowering, outgrowth**
effluent, **discharge, flow**
effodiant, **burrow**
effortless, **ease**
effulgent, **radiance, shining**
effusive, **gushing, overflow, pouring**
egal, **equality**
egalitarian, **equality**
egocentric, **attention**
egoistic, **concentration**
egolatrous, **self**
egotistic, **concentration**
egressive, **exit**
eident, **diligence**

Index

epigenetic, **cell**
epigonal, **Tiahuanaco**
epigonic, **Tiahuanaco, imitation**
epigrammatic, **inscription**
epigraphic, **inscription**
epilemmal, **nerve**
epinician, **victory**
epiphloedal, **bark, lichen**
epiphloedic, **bark, lichen**
episcopal, **bishop**
episodic, **incident**
epistatic, **control**
epistemic, **knowledge**
epistemologic, **knowledge**
epistemological, **knowledge**
epistemonic, **knowledge**
epistemophiliac, **knowledge**
epistographic, **correspondence**
epistolary, **correspondence**
epistolic, **correspondence**
epithalamial, **nuptial**
epithalamic, **nuptial, verse, marriage**
epithumetic, **appetite, desire**
epithymetic, **lust**
epithymetical, **lust**
epitomic, **peak**
epitomical, **peak**
epizoic, **parasite**
eponymic, **name**
eponymous, **name**
epoptic, **secret**
equilibrious, **balance**
equine, **horse**
equivocal, **ambiguity**
eremiophobic, **fear, self**
eremitic, **desert, recluse, solitude**
eremological, **desert**
eremophilous, **desert**
eremophobic, **fear, self**
erethic, **irritability, restlessness**
ergasiophobic, **fear, work**
ergatomorphic, **ant**
ergophilic, **work**
ergophobic, **fear, work**
eristic, **controversy, dispute**
eristical, **controversy**
erogenous, **desire**
erose, **unevenness**
erotophobic, **fear, sex**

errhine, **sneeze**
erroneous, **mistake**
ersatz, **substitution**
erubescent, **blush**
eruciform, **caterpillar**
eructative, **belch**
erudite, **knowledge**
eruginous, **verdigris**
erythrophobic, **fear, redness**
escalloped, **scale**
escharotic, **scar, scab**
esociform, **muskellunge, pickerel, pike**
esoteric, **novelty**
esotropic, **eye**
essential, **importance, necessity**
essorant, **soaring**
esthetic, **beauty, feeling**
estival, **summer**
esurient, **greed, hunger**
esurine, **acid**
eternal, **lasting**
eterne, **immortality**
ethereal, **heavens**
ethical, **morality**
ethmoid, **nasal cavity**
ethnic, **culture, race**
ethnical, **race**
ethnocratic, **race**
ethnologic, **culture**
ethnological, **culture**
ethological, **behavior**
etiolated, **whiteness**
etiologic, **cause**
etiological, **cause**
etymologic, **word**
etymological, **word**
eucrasic, **health**
eucratic, **health**
eucryphiaceous, **evergreen**
eudaemonic, **happiness**
eudemonical, **happiness**
eugenic, **breeding, improvement, race**
eulogic, **praise**
eulogious, **praise**
eulogistic, **praise**
eulogizing, **praise**
eunectic, **anaconda**

eupeptic, **cheerfulness, digestion**
euphemistic, **substitution, word**
euphonic, **harmony, sound**
euphonical, **sound**
euphonious, **sound**
euphoric, **happiness**
eupractic, **coordination**
euryalid, **starfish**
eurysomatic, **body**
Euskarian, **Basque**
eusuchian, **alligator, gavial**
Euterpean, **music**
euthanasic, **killing**
euthermic, **warmth**
euxine, **Black Sea**
evanid, **faintness**
even, **level**
eventful, **incident**
evil, **corruption, immorality, injury,
    lowness, malevolence, vileness**
eviternal, **eternity**
evocable, **calling**
evocatory, **calling**
exalate, **wing**
example, **illustration**
exappendiculate, **appendage**
exasperated, **annoyance, irritation**
excandence, **anger**
excandescence, **heat**
excandescent, **anger, heat**
excavate, **digging**
excavational, **digging**
excavatorial, **digging**
excellent, **superiority**
exceptional, **remarkability**
excessive, **exorbitance, extravagance,
    extremity, immoderation, in-
    ordinance**
excipient, **exception**
excoriate, **scrape**
excremental, **feces**
excrescent, **addition, extra**
exculpable, **innocence**
exculpatory, **pardon**
execratory, **curse**
exegetic, **Bible, explanation**
eximious, **excellence**
Exonian, **Exeter**
exorbitant, **abnormality, excess**
exordial, **beginning**

exoteric, **exterior, public**
exotropic, **eye**
expectorant, **spitting**
expirate, **utterance**
expiscatory, **search**
expletive, **filling**
expletory, **filling**
expositional, **explanation**
expulsatory, **expelling**
expulsive, **expelling**
exsanguine, **anemia, bloodlessness**
exsanguinous, **anemia, bloodlessness**
exsanguious, **bloodlessness**
extraforaneous, **outdoors**
extricable, **liberation**
extrinsic, **externality**
extrusive, **expulsion**
extrusory, **expulsion**
exudative, **sweat**
exudatory, **sweat**
exulcerate, **inflammation**
exuviable, **shedding**
exuvial, **molting, skin**

F

fabaceous, **bean**
fabiform, **bean**
fabled, **legend, myth**
fabricated, **forgery**
fabricative, **invention**
fabular, **fable**
fabulous, **fable, legend, myth**
façadal, **front**
facetious, **humor, joker**
facial, **face, front**
facical, **whimsy**
facinorous, **wickedness**
facsimile, **copy, imitation**
fact-finding, **evaluation**
factional, **clique, combination, party**
factionary, **clique, combination,
    party**
factious, **clique, combination, dis-
    sent, party**

factitive, **verb**
factitudinous, **reality**
factive, **making**
facund, **eloquence**
fainéant, **idleness, inactivity**
faithful, **belief**
faithless, **infidelity**
fake, **counterfeit, imitation**
falcate, **hook, scythe, sickle**
falcated, **curve, hook**
falciform, **scythe, sickle**
falcular, **scythe, sickle**
fallacious, **deception, error, fraud**
fall-down, **turn**
fallible, **deception, error, fraud**
fallow, **cultivation**
Falstaffian, **braggart, impudence, wit**
familial, **heredity**
familiar, **acquaintance, intimacy**
famous, **celebrity, notoriety**
fanatic, **enthusiasm, frenzy, madness, zeal**
fanatical, **enthusiasm, frenzy, madness, zeal**
fanciful, **whimsy**
fancy, **whimsy**
fangled, **decoration**
fantastic, **imagination**
fantastical, **imagination**
farcical, **absurdity, humor**
farinaceous, **flour**
farraginous, **disorder, mix**
fascicular, **bundle**
fastigiate, **bundle**
fat, **obesity**
fatal, **death**
fatalistic, **acceptance, determinism**
fatidic, **prophecy**
fatidical, **prophecy**
fatuous, **foolishness**
fearful, **fright**
fearless, **intrepidity**
febrific, **fever**
febrile, **fever, heat**
febriphobic, **fear, fever**
fecal, **feces**
fecial, **diplomacy, treaty**
feculent, **excrement, feces, filth**
fecund, **fertility**

feldspathic, **feldspar**
feline, **cat**
felinophilic, **cat**
felinophobic, **cat, fear**
femicidal, **killing, woman**
feminine, **female, woman**
feministic, **woman**
femoral, **thigh**
fenestral, **window**
feracious, **abundance, fertility, fruit**
feral, **animal, death, taming**
ferial, **holiday**
ferric, **iron**
ferrous, **iron**
ferruginous, **rust**
fertile, **impregnation, prolificacy**
ferulaceous, **reed**
ferulic, **switch**
fervent, **boiling, burning**
Fescennine, **obscenity**
festal, **holiday**
festive, **holiday, revel**
festucine, **yellowness**
fetial, **diplomacy, treaty**
fetid, **smell, stench**
fetishistic, **idolatry**
feudal, **landholding, tenure**
feudalistic, **landholding, tenure**
feudatorial, **landholding, tenure**
feverish, **ague, heat**
fibular, **brooch**
ficiform, **fig**
ficoid, **fig**
fictile, **plastic, pottery**
fictional, **imagination**
fideistic, **faith**
fidicinal, **instrument**
fiduciary, **trust**
fiendish, **cruelty, savage, wickedness**
fierce, **anger, cruelty, savage, wickedness**
figuline, **clay**
filial, **daughter, son**
filical, **fern**
filicidal, **child, killing**
filiciform, **fern**
filiform, **filament, thread**
fimbrial, **fringe**
fimbriate, **fringe**

Index

G

Index

gregarian, crowd, flock, herd, mob
gregarious, crowd, flock, herd, mob
gremial, bosom, lap
gressorial, walking
grievous, burden, sorrow, suffering, weight
gripple, avarice, tenacity
griseous, grayness
grizzled, hair
grizzly, grayness, hair
gromatic, surveying
grossular, gooseberry
grossulariaceous, saxifrage
grotesque, incongruity, ugliness
grumose, grain, granule
grumous, blood
gubernative, government
gubernatorial, government, governor
guilty, culpability
gushing, effusiveness, teeming
gustable, taste
gustative, taste
guttate, drop
guttery, furrow, mire, mud
guttiferous, gum, resin
guttiform, droplet
guttular, droplet
guttulate, droplet
guttural, throat
gymnastic, exercise
gymnophobic, fear, nudity
gynarchic, government, woman
gynecian, woman
gynecic, woman
gynecoid, woman
gynecomorphous, female
gyneocratic, government, woman
gynephobic, fear, hatred, woman
gynic, woman
gynophobic, fear, hatred, woman
gypsyish, wanderer
gyral, brain
gyrate, coil, curve
gyratory, circle, spiral, vortex
gyrony, triangle
gyrous, circle, spiral, vortex

H

habilable, clothing
habilatory, clothing
habile, ability, expertise, skill, suitability
habilimental, clothing
habilimented, clothing
habit, consideration, holding
habited, clothing
habitual, custom, habit, regularity
habituate, custom, regularity
hacked, browbeating
hackney, hire, triteness
Hadean, underworld
haematal, blood
haematic, blood
haematopoietic, blood
haggard, exhaustion
hagiarchal, government
hagiographic, saint
hagiologic, saint
hagiological, saint
hagiophobic, dislike, saint
halcyon, peace
halcyonian, peace
halcyonic, peace
halieutic, fishing
Haligonian, Halifax
halimous, maritime
halinous, salt
haliographic, sea
haliotoid, abalone
hallowed, blessing, consecration
hallucinational, delusion, dream
hallucinative, delusion
hallucinatory, delusion, dream
haloid, salt
halt, limp
halting, lameness
hamacratic, government
hamadryadic, nymph
hamartiological, sin
hamartophobic, error, fear, sin
hamate, hook
hamated, hook
hamiform, hook
hamular, hook

hamulate, **hook**
hamulose, **hook**
hamulous, **hook**
hanced, **lintel**
handy, **convenience, deftness, skill, versatility**
haphephobic, **fear, touch**
happy, **joy**
haptephobic, **fear, touch**
haptic, **touch**
hard, **ardure, difficulty**
harish, **foolishness**
harlot, **lewdness, wantonness**
harmful, **hurtfulness, injury, mischief**
harmoniacal, **concordancy**
harmonial, **concordancy**
harmonic, **concordancy, music**
harmonical, **music**
harmonious, **concordancy, music**
harpactophagous, **predator**
harsh, **coarseness, rigor**
haruspical, **fortuneteller, prophecy, soothsayer**
haruspicate, **fortuneteller**
hastate, **arrow, spear**
haughty, **arrogance, disdain, pride, scorn**
haustellate, **sucker**
haustorial, **sucker**
hazardous, **chance, peril**
hazy, **fog, mist, obscurity**
heady, **violence, will**
heart-rending, **anguish, grief**
heart-sore, **anguish, grief**
hearty, **energy, health, warmth**
heavenly, **paradise**
heavy, **burden, weight**
hebamic, **maieutics, obstetrics**
hebdomadal, **seven, week**
hebetic, **puberty**
hebetudinous, **lethargy**
hectic, **excitement**
hectical, **excitement**
hedonic, **pleasure**
hedonistic, **pleasure**
hegemonic, **dominance, leadership**
hegemonical, **leadership**
heinous, **wickedness**

helcoid, **ulcer**
helcological, **ulcer**
heliac, **sun**
heliacal, **sun**
heliastic, **dicast**
helic, **screw**
helical, **coil, screw, spiral**
helicine, **spiral**
helicoid, **spiral**
heliocentric, **sun**
heliographic, **sun**
heliographical, **sun**
heliolatrous, **sun**
heliophilous, **sunlight**
heliophobic, **fear, sun**
Helladic, **Greece**
Hellenic, **Greece**
helminthic, **worm**
helminthophobic, **fear, worm**
helobious, **marsh**
helodes, **marsh**
helpful, **assistance**
Helvetian, **Switzerland**
Helvetic, **Switzerland**
hemal, **blood**
hematal, **blood**
hematic, **blood**
hematobic, **blood**
hematoid, **blood**
hematologic, **blood**
hematological, **blood**
hematophagous, **blood**
hematopoietic, **blood**
hematothermal, **mammal**
hemeralopic, **blindness, day**
hemic, **blood**
hemipteroid, **aphid, mealybug**
hemipterous, **aphid, mealybug**
hemoid, **blood**
hemopathological, **blood**
hemophiliac, **bleeding**
hemoptoic, **spitting**
hendecagonal, **side**
hepatic, **liver**
hepatological, **liver**
heptagonal, **seven, side**
heptahedral, **seven**
heptal, **seven**
herbivorous, **eating, plant**

Index

Homoousian, **identicality**
homopteran, **fly**
homopterous, **fly**
honest, **rectitude**
hordeiform, **barley**
horizontal, **flatness**
horologic, **clock, watch**
horological, **clock, timepiece, watch**
horologiographic, **timepiece**
horrendous, **fright**
hortative, **advice, advisor, encouragement**
hortatory, **advice, advisor, encouragement**
hoserriform, **saw**
hospitable, **friendliness**
hotauted, **tangle**
hovesicatory, **blister**
hued, **color**
huge, **giant**
hugger-mugger, **secret**
human, **mortal**
humane, **mercy, sympathy**
humectant, **diluent**
humeral, **shoulder**
humid, **moisture**
humific, **moisture**
humilific, **shyness**
humorific, **comedy**
humorous, **comedy**
hyalescent, **glass, transparency**
hyaline, **glass, transparency**
hyaloid, **glass**
hyalophobic, **fear, glass**
hyalopterous, **wing**
hydatiform, **cyst**
hydrographic, **water**
hydrographical, **water**
hydrologic, **water**
hydrological, **water**
hydromantic, **water**
hydropathic, **water**
hydrophobic, **fear, rabies, water**
hydrotherapeutical, **bathing**
hydrous, **water**
hyerbaric, **utility**
hyetal, **precipitation**

hyetological, **precipitation, rain**
hygenic, **cleanliness**
hygienic, **health**
hygrophilous, **water**
hygrophobic, **fear, liquid, water**
hylactic, **barking**
Hylean, **forest**
hylephobic, **dislike**
hylic, **matter**
hylophagous, **eating, wood**
hymenoid, **membrane**
hymneal, **marriage**
hypaethral, **outdoors**
hypengyophobic, **fear, responsibility**
hyperbolic, **exaggeration**
hyperboreal, **cold, north**
hyperborean, **Arctic, cold, Eskimo,
north, paradise**
hyperchordal, **spine**
hyperdulic, **Virgin Mary**
hypergamic, **marriage**
hypergamous, **marriage**
hypermetropic, **farsightedness**
hyperopic, **farsightedness**
hypertrophic, **development, growth**
hypethral, **outdoors**
hypnopedic, **sleep**
hypnophobic, **fear, sleep**
hypocoristic, **baby talk, name, suffix**
hypocritical, **deceit**
hypogeal, **subterrain**
hyponymic, **generic name, name**
hyponymous, **generic name, name**
hypothetical, **premise**
hypotrophic, **development, growth**
hypoxic, **oxygen**
hypsiliform, **Y**
hypsiloid, **upsilon, Y**
hypsiphobic, **fear, height**
hypsophobic, **fear, height**
hysterocystic, **bladder, uterus**
hysteroid, **boat**
hystricid, **porcupine**
hystricoid, **porcupine**
hystricomorph, **guinea pig**
hystricomorphic, **guinea pig**
hystricomorphous, **guinea pig**

Index

I

iambic, **foot**
iatric, **doctor, medicine**
iatroliptic, **friction**
iatrophobic, **doctor, fear**
Iberian, **Georgia, Portugal, Spain**
Iberic, **Portugal, Spain**
Icarian, **flying**
Icenic, **Boadicea**
ichneutic, **tracking**
ichnographic, **floor plan, map**
ichnological, **fossil**
ichthyal, **fish**
ichthyolatrous, **fish**
ichthyomantic, **fish**
ichthyomorphic, **fish**
ichthyophagian, **eating, fish**
ichthyophagous, **fish**
ichthyophobic, **fear, fish**
iconic, **likeness**
iconological, **image**
icosian, **twenty**
icosteid, **ragfish**
icosteine, **ragfish**
icteric, **jaundice**
icterical, **jaundice**
icterine, **blackbird, bobolink,
   meadowlark, oriole, yellowness**
icteroid, **yellowness**
icthyic, **fish**
icthyoid, **fish**
icthyoidal, **fish**
icthyomorphous, **fish**
ictic, **stress**
ictritious, **yellowness**
Idalian, **Aphrodite**
Idean, **Mt. Ida**
ideographic, **writing**
ideographical, **writing**
idiochromatic, **color**
idiomorphic, **form**
idiomorphous, **form**
idioplasmatic, **cell**
idioplasmic, **cell**
idiospastic, **cramp**
idiosyncratic, **character**

idiosyncratical, **character**
idolatrous, **worship**
idoneal, **appropriateness**
idoneous, **appropriateness, fitness,
   suitability**
Idumaean, **Edom**
Idumean, **Edom**
idyllic, **paradise, ruralism**
Ignatian, **Jesuit, Loyola**
igneous, **fire**
igniform, **fire**
ignigenous, **fire**
ignoble, **baseness, meanness**
ignominious, **humiliation**
Iguvine, **Umbria**
Iliadic, **verse**
ilicaceous, **holly**
ilicic, **holly**
illaudable, **censure**
illaudatory, **criticism**
illecebrous, **allure**
illusive, **deceit**
illusory, **deceit**
imbricate, **overlap**
immane, **atrocity, vastness**
immense, **hugeness**
immensive, **immeasurableness**
imperate, **command**
imperatorial, **emperor**
imperious, **arrogance, dominance**
impertinent, **forwardness**
impetrative, **entreaty**
impetratory, **entreaty**
implacental, **monotreme**
implacentate, **monotreme**
implicate, **tangle**
impolite, **incivility**
importunate, **harassment, urgency**
imposterous, **deceit**
impostrous, **deceit**
imprecatory, **curse**
impubic, **behavior**
imsonic, **onomatopoeia**
inane, **absurdity, farce**
incalescent, **warmth**
incandescent, **glow**
incantational, **chanting**
incantatory, **chanting**
incarnadine, **redness**

J

juberous, **doubt, hesitation**
jubilean, **celebration**
Judaean, **Jews**
Judaic, **Jews**
Judaical, **Jews**
Judas-colored, **hair**
Judean, **Jews**
judicial, **decision**
judicious, **decision**
jugal, **marriage**
jugate, **overlap, pair**
juglandaceous, **walnut**
jugular, **neck, throat**
juicy, **moisture, succulence**
jujuistic, **sorcery**
Julian, **Caesar, Julius**
jumbled, **confusion, incoherency**
jumbly, **confusion**
jumbo, **hugeness**
jumpy, **nervousness**
juncaceous, **rush**
junciform, **rush**
junelle, **twin**
jungly, **vegetation**
junior, **youth**
Junoesque, **beauty, voluptuousness**
jural, **obligation**
juratory, **expression, oath**
jussive, **command**
just, **correctness**
justiciable, **liability**
juvenal, **youth**
juvenescent, **youth**
juvenile, **youth**
juxtaposed, **adjacency**

K

Kafuan, **tool**
kakistcratic, **government**
kakorrhaphiophobic, **failure, fear**
kaligenous, **alkali**
Kamikaze, **suicide**
kaolinic, **clay**
karmic, **determinism, fate**

Kartvelian, **Georgia**
karyoclastic, **disintegration**
karyogamic, **fusion**
karyologic, **cell, nucleus**
karyological, **cell, nucleus**
karyotic, **nucleus**
katabatic, **motion**
keen, **edge**
kenophobic, **fear, space**
keratinous, **horn**
keratogenic, **horn**
keratogenous, **horn**
keratoid, **horn**
keraunomantic, **thunder**
keraunophobic, **fear, lightning, thunder**
keraunoscopic, **thunder**
kickish, **irritation**
kid, **youth**
kindhearted, **sympathy**
kindred, **similarity**
kinematic, **motion**
kinesic, **gesture, motion**
kinesodic, **conveyance**
kinesthetic, **motion**
kinetic, **motion**
kinetical, **motion**
kinetogenic, **motion**
kingly, **importance, master**
kinofluous, **astringent**
Kiplingese, **imperialism**
kirtled, **tunic**
kismetic, **fate**
Kit-cat, **Whig Club**
kitchen, **cookery**
kithogue, **hand**
kitling, **cat, inexperience**
kitthoge, **hand**
kittle, **management**
Kleistian, **Leyden Jar**
kleptic, **thief**
kleptistic, **burglary, thief**
kleptomaniac, **thief**
kleptomaniacal, **stealing**
kleptophobic, **fear, stealing, thief**
knappish, **spite**
knarred, **knot**
knarry, **knot**
knavish, **vulgarity**

L

lacustrian, **lake**
lacustrine, **coast, lake**
laden, **burden, load**
laetic, **cultivator**
lageniform, **flask**
laggard, **slowness**
lagomorphic, **pika, rabbit**
lagoonal, **channel, lake, pond**
lagopous, **rabbit**
laic, **secularity**
lairdly, **tenant**
lairy, **filth, mire**
laissez-faire, **inactivity, individuality, tolerance**
laliophobic, **fear, talk**
Lallan, **lowlands**
lalophobic, **fear, talk**
lambent, **flicker, glide**
lambitive, **lick**
lame, **disability, infirmity**
lamellar, **membrane, plate, sheet, spar**
lamelliform, **membrane, plate, sheet**
lamentable, **mourning, sorrow**
lamentational, **mourning, sorrow**
lamentatory, **jeremiad, mourning, sorrow**
lamented, **mourning, sorrow**
lamentive, **mourning, sorrow**
laminable, **scale, flake, layer**
laminar, **flake, layer, membrane, plate, scale, sheet**
laminary, **flake, layer, scale**
laminate, **flake, layer, scale, sheet**
laminated, **flake, layer, scale**
laminose, **flake, layer, plate, scale, sheet**
lamish, **disability, infirmity**
lammate, **plate**
lammose, **membrane**
lamping, **brilliance, flash**
lampyrid, **firefly, glowworm**
lanate, **wool**
lanated, **wool**
lanceolate, **point**
lanceolated, **point**
lane-born, **birth**
langued, **tongue**
languent, **fatigue, sickness, weakness**
languescent, **fatigue, sickness, sluggishness, weakness**
languid, **fatigue, sickness, sluggishness, weakness**
languishing, **fatigue, sickness, weakness**
languorous, **grief, sorrow**
lank, **thinness**
lanky, **thinness**
lanose, **wool**
lanuginous, **down**
Laodicean, **indifference**
lapactic, **catharsis, laxative**
lapidarian, **engraving, gem**
lapidary, **gem**
lapideous, **gem**
lapidescent, **petrification**
lapidicolous, **stone**
lapidific, **gem**
lapidose, **gem**
lapilliform, **gem**
lapsed, **neglect**
lapsing, **neglect**
laquearian, **noose**
larcenic, **theft**
larcenish, **theft**
larcenous, **theft**
lardaceous, **fat**
large, **amplitude, bulk**
largifical, **amplitude, bulk**
larid, **gull, tern**
larine, **gull**
larithmic, **population**
laroid, **gull, seagull**
larrikin, **behavior**
larrikinism, **loafer**
larval, **worm**
larvate, **concealment, mask, obscurity**
lascivious, **immorality**
lasslorn, **forsaking**
last, **finality, ultimatum**
lasting, **permanence**
late, **tardiness**
latebricole, **hole**
latemose, **ultimatum**
latemost, **finality**
latent, **dormancy, hiding**
lateral, **side**

latericeous, **brick**
lateritious, **brick**
latescent, **dormancy, hiding**
latesome, **tardiness**
latest, **finality, ultimatum**
lathen, **wood**
laticiferous, **latex**
laticostate, **rib**
latidentate, **tooth**
latinostral, **beak**
latipennate, **wing**
latirostrous, **beak**
latish, **tardiness**
laudable, **praise**
laudative, **praise**
laudatory, **praise**
lauraceous, **sassafras**
laureate, **honor**
laurel, **honor**
lautitious, **sumptuousness**
lava, **fluid**
lavatic, **fluid**
lavational, **cleansing, washing**
lavatory, **cleansing, washing**
lavered, **plowshare**
lavic, **fluid**
lavish, **bestowal, bounty, extravagance, munificence**
lavishing, **bestowal, bounty, extravagance**
lazarly, **leper, sore**
lazarous, **leper, sore**
lazuline, **blueness**
lazy, **action, exertion**
lea, **fallowness**
leal, **loyalty, truth**
leathwake, **suppleness**
lecanomantic, **water**
lecherous, **lewdness, lust**
lecithal, **yolk**
lecithic, **yolk**
lectual, **confinement**
leer, **void**
legal, **authorization, law, legitimacy**
legative, **deputy**
legatorial, **legacy, testator**
legendary, **tradition**
legendic, **tradition**
legific, **law**

legitimate, **reality**
legitime, **reality**
leguminiform, **bean, pea**
leguminose, **bean, pea**
leguminous, **alfalfa, bean, pea**
leisurable, **recreation**
leisured, **recreation, unemployment**
lemnaceous, **duckweed**
lemuroid, **tarsier**
lenient, **clemency, mercy**
lenitive, **clemency, mercy**
lentibulariaceous, **bladderwort**
lentic, **water**
lenticular, **freckle**
lenticulate, **freckle**
lentiform, **freckle**
lentigenous, **freckle**
lentous, **viscosity**
leontocephalous, **head**
lepadoid, **barnacle**
lepid, **wit**
lepidopteral, **butterfly, moth**
lepidopterous, **butterfly, moth**
lepismid, **silverfish**
lepisosteid, **silverfish**
leporid, **hare, rabbit**
leporiform, **hare, rabbit**
leporine, **hare, rabbit**
lepraphobic, **fear, leprosy**
leprose, **scale**
leptasomatic, **body**
leptasomic, **body**
leptodactylous, **toe**
leptorrhinian, **nose**
lered, **learning**
lesbian, **homosexuality**
lethal, **death, fatality, mortality**
lethargic, **drowsiness, fatigue, sleep**
Lethean, **forgetfulness**
lethiferous, **death**
leucochroic, **complexion**
leucopenic, **white cell deficiency**
leucospheric, **corona**
leukopenic, **white cell deficiency**
leviable, **assessment, tax**
levigable **lightening**
levigate, **smoothness**
lew, **tepidness**
lewd, **indecency**

lexical, **vocabulary, word**
lexicographic, **dictionary**
lexicographical, **dictionary**
lexicologic, **word**
lexicological, **word**
lexigraphic, **dictionary**
lexiphanic, **bombasticism, language**
liable, **responsibility**
libaniferous, **incense**
libanophorous, **incense**
libanotophorous, **incense**
libatory, **pouring**
libellulid, **dragonfly**
liberal, **generosity, munificence**
liberticidal, **freedom**
libertine, **behavior**
licentious, **immorality, orgy**
lienal, **spleen**
lienteric, **food**
ligenous, **wood**
light, **brightness**
lignescent, **wood**
ligniform, **wood**
ligular, **tongue**
ligulate, **tongue**
liguloid, **tongue**
like, **similarity**
liliaceous, **garlic, onion**
Lilliputian, **pygmy, smallness**
lily-livered, **coward**
limacine, **slug**
limacoid, **slug**
limbate, **color**
limber, **pliancy**
limbic, **border**
limbiferous, **border, margin**
limicoline, **coast, shore**
limicolous, **mud**
liminal, **threshhold**
liminary, **threshhold**
limitative, **restriction**
limivorous, **mud**
limnetic, **water**
limniadic, **nymph**
limnologic, **water**
limnological, **water**
limous, **mud, slime**
limp, **slackness**
limuloid, **horseshoe crab**

linguacious, **loquacity**
lingual, **tongue**
linguiform, **tongue**
linguistic, **language**
linguistical, **language**
lingulate, **strap, tongue**
Linnean, **classification**
liparoid, **fat, obesity**
liparous, **fat, obesity**
lipogenous, **fat, obesity**
lipoid, **fat**
liquid, **fluid**
lirate, **ridge**
lish, **activity**
lissencephalic, **brain**
lissotrichous, **hair**
literal, **letter, writing**
lithic, **stone**
lithochromic, **stone**
lithodomous, **rock**
lithoglyptic, **engraving**
lithographic, **stone**
lithoid, **stone**
lithoidal, **stone**
lithoidolatrous, **rock**
lithoidological, **rock**
lithologic, **geology**
lithological, **geology**
lithomantic, **rock**
litigious, **behavior, dispute, law,
  quarrel**
littoral, **coast, seashore, shore**
liturate, **spot**
liturgical, **worship**
lobbish, **clown**
local, **place**
lochetic, **ambush**
lochy, **lake**
locular, **box, cavity, cell, chamber**
lofty, **height**
logographic, **speech**
logogriphic, **anagram**
logolatrous, **word**
logomachic, **word**
logomachical, **word**
logomantic, **word**
logopedic, **speech**
logorrheic, **talkativeness, wordiness**
lonely, **company**

M

madid, **moisture, wetness**
madreporian, **coral**
madreporic, **coral**
madrigalian, **lyric**
mafic, **magnesium**
mageiric, **magician**
magical, **enchantment**
magiric, **cookery**
magnaminous, **generosity**
magnanime, **generosity**
maieutic, **knowledge, obstetrics**
maimed, **mutilation**
majestic, **magnificence, royalty,**
  splendor
malaceous, **pear**
malacological, **mollusk**
malacotic, **softness**
malactic, **emollient**
maladive, **sickness**
maladroit, **clumsiness**
malapert, **impudence**
malar, **cheek**
male, **masculinity**
maledicent, **slander**
maledictive, **slander**
maledictory, **curse, slander**
malefactory, **evil**
malefic, **evil**
maleficent, **evil**
maleficial, **evil**
maleficiate, **evil**
malevolent, **anger, evil, hatred**
malevolous, **evil**
malfeasant, **criminal**
malicious, **evil**
maliferous, **evil**
maliform, **apple**
malignant, **evil**
malleiform, **hammer**
malodorant, **stench**
malodorous, **smell, stench**
mammary, **breast**
mammiferous, **breast**
mammiform, **breast**
mammillar, **nipple**
mammillary, **nipple**
mammillate, **nipple**
mammilliform, **nipple**
mammilloid, **nipple**

mammonish, **greed**
manageable, **compliancy, control**
manal, **hand**
mancipative, **slavery**
Mancunian, **Manchester**
mandative, **command**
mandatory, **command, order**
mandibular, **jaw**
mandibulary, **jaw**
manducatory, **chewing**
manerial, **manor**
manganic, **manganese**
maniaphobic, **fear, insanity**
manid, **pangolin**
mantic, **divination**
manual, **hand**
marantic, **emaciation, starvation**
marasmic, **emaciation, starvation**
marasmoid, **starvation**
marasmous, **emaciation, starvation**
marcid, **decay, withering**
maremmatic, **swamp**
mare-rode, **nightmare**
marfire, **phosphorescence**
margaric, **pearl**
maricolous, **sea**
marinal, **sea**
marine, **navigation, ocean, sea**
Mariological, **Virgin Mary**
Marist, **Virgin Mary**
mariticidal, **husband, killing**
maritime, **navigation, ocean**
marmoreal, **marble**
marsupial, **pouch**
martial, **war**
mascled, **lozenge**
massaline, **silk**
mastic, **adhesion**
masticatory, **chewing**
masticurous, **stingray**
mastigate, **flagellum**
mastigophoric, **flagellum**
mastigote, **flagellum**
mataeological, **speechmaking**
maternal, **mother**
mathetic, **science**
matinal, **morning**
matriarchal, **government, mother**
matriarchic, **mother**

matriarchical, **mother**
matrical, **uterus, womb**
matricidal, **killing, mother**
matricular, **uterus, womb**
matrilineal, **inheritance**
matrilinear, **inheritance**
matrimonial, **marriage**
matripotestal, **mother**
matronymic, **name**
matutinal, **morning**
maudlin, **behavior, sentimentality**
mawkish, **sentimentality**
maxillar, **jaw**
maxillary, **jaw**
maximistic, **proverb**
mecopterous, **fly**
medianic, **seer**
medianimic, **seer**
medullary, **marrow**
megachiropteran, **fruit bat**
megachiropterous, **fruit bat**
megalopic, **eye**
megascopic, **magnification**
megaseismic, **earthquake**
meiotic, **understatement**
melancholic, **gloom**
melanian, **skin**
melanic, **pigmentation, skin**
melaniferous, **black pigment**
melanochroous, **skin**
melanocomous, **complexion, hair**
melanodermic, **skin**
melanoid, **pigmentation**
melanotrichous, **hair**
melanous, **complexion**
melilotic, **sweet clover**
meline, **yellowness**
meliorist, **improvement**
melioristic, **improvement**
melittological, **bee**
mellifluous, **smoothness**
mellisugent, **nectar**
mellivorous, **nectar**
melopoeic, **melody**
melopoetic, **melody**
membracid, **treehopper**
membracine, **treehopper**
mendacious, **lying**
mendicant, **begging**

menial, **servant**
menorrheic, **menstruation**
mensal, **table**
mensual, **month**
mensural, **measurement, month**
mensurative, **month**
mephitic, **smell, stench**
mercenary, **profit**
meridional, **south**
meristic, **segment**
merogenetic, **segment**
meropic, **blindness**
merry, **happiness, pleasure**
mertricious, **prostitute**
mesal, **middle**
mesaticephalic, **head**
mesencephalic, **midbrain**
mesial, **middle**
mesmeric, **hypnosis**
mesmerizing, **hypnosis**
mesomorphic, **athlete, body**
mesothetic, **middle**
metachronic, **chronology**
metagraphic, **transliteration**
metaphrastic, **translation**
metaphrastical, **translation**
metastatic, **change, transformation**
metempsychic, **soul**
metempsychosic, **soul**
metempsychosical, **soul**
metonymic, **name**
metonymical, **name**
metopic, **forehead**
metopomantic, **face**
metric, **measurement**
metrical, **measurement, stress**
metrological, **measurement**
metronymic, **mother, name**
metropolitan, **city**
mettlesome, **courage**
miasmic, **smog**
miasmological, **air**
microcephalic, **head**
microcephalous, **head**
microceratous, **antennae**
microlecithal, **yolk**
micrologic, **classification**
microseismic, **earthquake**
microstomatous, **mouth**

nihilitic, **nothingness**
nimbiferous, **storm**
nimble, **adroitness, cleverness**
nimbose, **cloud, storm**
nimbused, **atmosphere, halo, vapor**
nimious, **excess, extravagance**
Niobean, **pride**
nippitate, **ale**
nirvanic, **paradise**
nitid, **brightness, effulgence, gloss,
    sheen, shining**
nitidous, **brightness, gloss**
nival, **snow**
niveous, **snow, whiteness**
nivicolous, **snow**
Noachian, **Noah**
Noachic, **Noah**
Noachical, **Noah**
Noaic, **Noah**
nobiliary, **aristocrat**
nocent, **criminal, guilt**
nociceptive, **pain**
noctambulant, **sleepwalking**
noctambulic, **sleepwalking**
noctambulistic, **sleepwalking**
noctambulous, **sleepwalking**
noctidiurnal, **day**
noctilucent, **cloud, glow**
noctilucous, **phosphorescence**
noctiphobic, **fear, night**
nocturnal, **evening, night**
nocuous, **hurtfulness**
nodated, **knot**
noddy, **sleep**
noded, **knot**
nodiform, **knot**
nodose, **knot**
nodous, **knot**
nodulose, **knob**
noetic, **intellect, mind, reasoning**
noggen, **hemp**
noily, **wool**
noiseful, **sound**
noisome, **annoyance, disgust, harm,
    stench**
noisy, **sound**
nomadic, **wandering**
nomenclative, **name**
nomenclatorial, **catalogue, dictionary,
    glossary, list, name, register**

nomenclatural, **catalogue, designa-
    tion, dictionary, glossary, list,
    name, register**
nomic, **custom, natural law, validity**
nominative, **name**
nomographic, **law**
nomographical, **law**
nomological, **law, legislation**
nomothetic, **law, universality**
nonagesimal, **ninety**
nonagonal, **side**
nonuple, **nine**
nooklike, **corner**
noological, **understanding**
nooscopic, **mind**
no-par, **value**
Nordic, **Scandinavia**
normal, **model, pattern, standard,
    type**
normative, **model, pattern, standard,
    type**
nosologic, **disease**
nosological, **disease**
nosophobic, **disease, fear**
nostologic, **aging**
nostriled, **nose**
nosy, **fragrance**
notaphilic, **banknote**
notational, **music**
notional, **idea**
notommatid, **rotifer**
notoryctid, **mole**
nought, **invalidity**
noumenal, **reality**
Novanglian, **New England**
Novanglican, **New England**
novation, **revolution**
Novemberish, **dreariness**
novenary, **nine**
novene, **nine**
novennial, **year**
novercal, **stepmother**
novilunar, **moon**
novitial, **neophyte, novice, postulant**
nowy, **curve**
noxious, **harm, hurtfulness, injury**
nubile, **girl**
nubilous, **cloud, fog, mist**

O

obstetrical, **childbirth**
obstreperous, **clamor, noise**
obstruent, **blocking**
obtect, **cover**
obtected, **cover**
obumbrant, **overhang**
obumbrate, **darkening**
obviable, **forestalling, preclusion**
obvolent, **curve**
occasional, **infrequency**
occasive, **sun, west**
Occidental, **west**
occludent, **obstruction**
occlusal, **bite**
occluse, **closing**
occlusive, **closing**
oceanic, **sea**
oceanographic, **sea**
oceanographical, **sea**
ocellar, **eye, spot**
ocellated, **eye**
ocellation, **spot**
ochlocratic, **government, mob**
ochlocratical, **government, mob**
ochlophobic, **crowd, fear, mob**
ocreated, **boots, leggings**
ocreclte, **boots, leggings**
octad, **eight**
octadic, **eight**
octagonal, **side**
octal, **eight**
octamerous, **eight**
octennial, **year**
octuple, **eight**
octuplet, **eight**
octuplex, **eight**
octuplicate, **eight**
ocular, **eye**
oculauditory, **sight and hearing**
odd, **matching**
odonate, **damselfly, dragonfly**
odontalgic, **tooth, toothache**
odontographic, **tooth**
odontological, **tooth**
odontophobic, **fear, tooth**
odorate, **scent**
odoriferant, **scent**
odoriferous, **fragrance, scent**
odorific, **scent**

odynophobic, **fear, pain**
oecodomic, **architecture**
oecodomical, **architecture**
oecophobic, **fear, home**
oecumenic, **church**
oecumenical, **church**
oenological, **wine**
oenomantic, **wine**
oenophilic, **wine**
oenophobic, **fear, hatred, wine**
oenopoetic, **wine**
oestrid, **botfly**
ogreish, **behavior**
oikophobic, **fear, home**
oinomantic, **wine**
oinophilic, **wine**
oinophobic, **fear, hatred, wine**
oleaginous, **lard, oil**
olecranal, **elbow**
olecranial, **elbow**
olecranioid, **elbow**
olefiant, **ethylene**
oleiferous, **oil**
oleose, **oil**
oleous, **oil**
oleraceous, **potherb**
olfactological, **odor**
olfactophobic, **smell, fear, odor**
olfactory, **odor, smell**
oligarchic, **government**
oligarchical, **government**
oligophrenic, **deficiency**
ombrological, **rain**
ombrophilic, **rain**
ombrophilous, **rain**
ombrophobic, **fear, rain**
ombrophobus, **rain**
ominous, **evil, omen, portend**
omissible, **neglect**
omissive, **neglect**
ommateal, **eye**
ommatophobic, **eye, fear**
omniscient, **knowledge, sagacity**
omnivorous, **eating**
omophagic, **flesh**
omophagous, **eating, flesh**
omphalic, **navel, umbilicus**
onanistic, **masturbation**
oncologic, **tumor**

orificial, **opening**
original, **beginning, ingenuity**
originary, **cause**
orismologic, **word**
orismological, **word**
ornamental, **adornment, decoration**
ornamentary, **adornment, decoration**
ornate, **adornment, decoration**
ornithic, **bird**
ornithologic, **bird**
ornithological, **bird**
ornithomantic, **bird**
ornithophilous, **bird**
orofacial, **mouth**
orogenetic, **mountain**
orogenic, **mountain**
orographic, **geography**
orographical, **geography**
orological, **mountain**
orometric, **mountain**
orophilous, **subalpine**
orotund, **resonance**
orphic, **mystic, oracle**
orthian, **pitch**
orthoëpic, **pronunciation**
orthoëpical, **pronunciation**
orthoëpistic, **pronunciation**
orthogonal, **right**
orthographic, **spelling, writing**
orthological, **language**
orthoptic, **vision**
orthostatic, **standing**
oryzivorous, **eating, rice**
oscheal, **scrotum**
oscillatory, **wavering**
oscitant, **drowsiness, stupidity, yawn**
osculant, **kiss**
oscular, **kiss, mouth**
osculate, **kiss**
osculatory, **kiss**
osmatic, **odor**
osmetic, **smell**
osmic, **odor**
osmidrotic, **perspiration**
osmological, **odor**
osmonological, **odor**
osmophobic, **fear, odor**
osphresiophilic, **odor**
osphresiophobic, **dislike, odor**
osphretic, **odor, smell**

osseous, **bone**
ossiferous, **bone**
ossific, **bone**
osteal, **skeleton**
ostensible, **exhibition**
ostensive, **exhibition**
ostentatious, **pretention**
osteographic, **bone**
osteographical, **bone**
osteologic, **bone**
osteological, **bone**
osteomantic, **bone, divination**
osteopathic, **bone**
osteopathological, **bone**
ostiolar, **opening, pore**
ostracean, **oyster**
ostraceous, **oyster**
ostracine, **oyster**
ostreiform, **oyster**
ostreoid, **oyster**
ostrephagous, **eating, oyster**
otalgic, **earache**
otiatric, **ear**
otic, **ear**
otiose, **futility, leisure, sterility, unemployment**
otitic, **ear**
otologic, **ear**
otological, **ear**
otorhinal, **ear**
ovarian, **coast**
ovarious, **egg**
ovate, **egg**
ovine, **sheep**
ovoid, **egg**
ovoidal, **egg**
ovular, **egg**
ovulate, **egg**
Oxonian, **Oxford**
oxypetalous, **petal**
oxyrhynchous, **beak**

P

pabular, **nourishment**

pantologic, **everything, knowledge**
pantological, **everything, knowledge**
pantometric, **measurement**
pantometrical, **measurement**
pantophagous, **eating**
papal, **pope**
papaphobic, **fear, pope**
papaveraceous, **opium, poppy**
papaverous, **opium**
paphian, **erotica, wantonness**
papilionaceous, **butterfly**
papilionid, **butterfly**
papolatrous, **pope**
pappose, **down**
papular, **food, pimple, sustenance**
papuliferous, **pimple**
papyraceous, **paper**
papyrological, **manuscript**
parachronic, **chronology**
paracoxurine, **palm civet**
paradigmatic, **model, pattern**
paradisaeid, **bird of paradise, bower-bird**
paradisean, **bird of paradise**
paradromic, **parallelism**
paragogic, **pronunciation**
paragogical, **pronunciation**
paralipophobic, **fear, negligence**
paramuthetic, **consolation**
paranasal, **nose**
paranephric, **adrenal gland**
paranoiac, **disorder**
paraphobic, **fear**
paraphrenic, **paranoia**
parasitic, **dependency**
parietal, **wall**
parine, **titmouse**
parisological, **equivocation, word**
parlous, **danger, hazard, risk**
parochial, **narrowmindedness, parish**
parodic, **imitation**
parodical, **imitation**
parodistic, **satire**
paroemiac, **aphorism, proverb**
paroemiographical, **aphorism, proverb**
paroemiological, **aphorism, proverb**
paronomastic, **pun**
parotitic, **mumps**

parous, **pregnancy**
parricidal, **father, killing**
partatile, **carrying**
particular, **part, portion**
particularistic, **part, portion**
partisan, **favoritism**
parturient, **birth, childbirth, fructification**
parturitive, **childbirth**
Paschal, **Easter**
pascual, **pasture**
pascuous, **pasture**
pashmina, **wool**
pasigraphic, **artificial language, language**
pasquilant, **lampoon**
pasquilic, **lampoon**
passant, **walking**
passeriform, **sparrow**
passerine, **sparrow**
passional, **emotion, feeling**
passionate, **emotion, feeling**
pastoral, **herdsman, ruralism, shepherd**
pastose, **paint**
patellate, **pan**
patelliform, **saucer**
paternal, **father**
pathetic, **emotion, feeling, pity, sorrow**
pathetical, **emotion, feeling, pity, sorrow**
pathic, **suffering**
pathognomic, **emotion**
pathological, **illness**
pathophobic, **disease, fear**
patibulate, **gallows**
patriarchal, **father, government**
patriarchic, **father**
patriarchical, **father**
patricidal, **father, killing**
patriclinous, **father**
patrilateral, **father**
patrilineal, **inheritance**
patrilinear, **inheritance**
patristic, **father**
patristical, **father**
patrologic, **Church Fathers, theology**

phlebotomical, **vein**
phlegmatic, **spirit**
phlogistic, **fire**
phobotactic, **trial and error**
phocine, **seal**
phoenicopteroid, **flamingo**
phoenicopterous, **flamingo**
phonetic, **sound**
phonetical, **sound**
phonic, **sound**
phonocamptic, **echo, sound**
phonogramic, **sound**
phonogrammic, **sound**
phonographic, **spelling**
phonographical, **spelling**
phonophobic, **fear, noise**
phorological, **epidemic**
photic, **light**
photological, **light**
photolytic, **decomposition**
photophobic, **fear, light**
phraseological, **vocabulary**
phratic, **well**
phrenetic, **frenzy, insanity**
phrenic, **diaphragm, mind**
phrenological, **skull**
phthisic, **consumption, tuberculosis, weakness**
phthisical, **consumption**
phthisicky, **tuberculosis**
phthisiophobic, **fear**
phthoric, **fluorine**
phycologic, **algae**
phyletic, **race, species**
phylloid, **leaf**
phylogenetic, **race**
phylogenetical, **race**
phylogenic, **race**
physalian, **Portuguese man-of-war**
physeterid, **whale**
physeteroid, **whale**
physiognomic, **face**
physiolatrous, **nature**
physiosophic, **nature**
physiosophical, **nature**
physiurgic, **nature**
phytivorous, **eating**
phytophagous, **eating, plant**
phytophilous, **plant**

piacular, **sacrifice, sin**
piazzaed, **square**
picaresque, **rascal, rogue**
piceous, **pitch**
piciform, **barbet, puffbird, toucan, woodpecker**
picine, **woodpecker**
pictorial, **illustration, painting, picture**
pierid, **butterfly**
pigheaded, **obstinacy**
pignorate, **pledge**
pignoratitious, **pledge**
pileate, **crest**
pileous, **hair**
pilgarlicky, **hair**
piliferous, **hair**
piliform, **hair**
piline, **hair**
pimply, **pustule**
pinguedinous, **obesity**
pinguescent, **obesity**
pinguid, **fat, obesity, portliness**
pinguified, **grease**
pinguinitescent, **grease**
pinguitudinous, **obesity**
pinnate, **feather**
pinnated, **feather**
pinnatifid, **feather**
piperaceous, **pepper**
piquant, **provocation**
piscatological, **fishing**
piscatorial, **fishing**
piscatory, **fisherman, fishing**
pisciform, **fish**
piscine, **fish**
piscivorous, **fish**
pisiform, **pea**
pistic, **faith**
pistological, **faith**
pit-headed, **viper**
pithecan, **anthropoid, ape**
pithecoid, **monkey**
pithecometric, **skeleton**
pithecomorphic, **anthropoid, ape**
placoid, **plate**
plagal, **melody**
plagiaristic, **stealing**
plaguy, **disease**

probable, **likelihood**
proboscidal, **nose, trunk**
proboscidate, **nose, trunk**
proboscidean, **trunk**
proboscidial, **nose, trunk**
proboscidian, **trunk**
proboscidiferous, **nose, trunk**
proboscidiform, **nose, trunk**
procellariid, **albatross, petrel, shear-water**
procellariiform, **albatross, petrel, shearwater**
procellous, **storm**
processional, **progression**
procrastinating, **dilatoriness**
procrastinative, **dilatoriness**
procrastinatory, **dilatoriness**
proctologic, **anus, rectum**
proctological, **anus, rectum**
prodigious, **omen**
proditorious, **betrayal**
prodromal, **precursor**
prodromic, **precursor**
professional, **occupation**
proficuous, **usefulness**
profit, **remuneration**
profligate, **vice**
profluent, **flow**
profluvious, **extravagance**
profugate, **fugitive**
profulgent, **shining**
prognathic, **projection**
prognathous, **projection**
prognostic, **omen**
prognosticative, **forecast, prophecy**
progredient, **progression**
projection, **jaw**
projicient, **projection**
prolate, **extension**
prolative, **prediction**
prolegomenal, **preface**
prolegomenous, **preface**
proleptical, **time**
prolicidal, **infant, killing**
proliferant, **production**
proliferative, **production**
prolific, **production, reproduction**
prolifical, **production**
prolix, **wordiness**

prone, **recumbency**
propaedeutic, **preparation**
propense, **leaning**
prophetic, **future, oracle**
prophylactic, **prevention**
propinquitous, **nearness, proximity**
propinquous, **nearness, proximity**
propitiable, **pacification**
propitial, **pacification**
propitiative, **pacification**
Propontic, **Sea of Marmara**
proprietorial, **ownership**
prosodic, **verse**
prosodical, **verse**
prosographic, **face**
prosopic, **face**
protelid, **aardwolf**
protolithic, **stone age**
protomorphic, **primitiveness**
protreptic, **encouragement, persuasion**
proverbiological, **aphorism**
provident, **foresight**
proximal, **nearness**
proximate, **closeness**
pruinate, **dust, frost**
pruinose, **dust, frost**
pruinous, **dust, frost**
pruniform, **plum**
prurient, **immorality**
pruriginous, **itch**
psammologic, **sand**
psammophilous, **sand**
psammophytic, **sand**
psammous, **sand**
pseudepigraphal, **authorship**
pseudepigraphic, **authorship**
pseudepigraphical, **authorship**
pseudepigraphous, **authorship**
pseudomaniacal, **lying**
pseudomantic, **divination**
psittaceous, **parrot**
psittacine, **macaw, parakeet, parrot**
psoatic, **tenderloin**
psocid, **book louse**
psocine, **book louse**
psoric, **psoriasis**
psychagogic, **persuasion**
psychic, **mind, soul**

Q

quadrifid, **four, lobe**
quadrifilar, **thread**
quadrilateral, **side**
quadrivial, **crossroads**
quadrivoltine, **silkworm**
quadruped, **feet**
quadrupedal, **feet**
quadruple, **four**
quadruplex, **four**
quadruplicate, **four**
quaestuary, **gain, profit**
quaggy, **bog**
qualmish, **nausea**
quashy, **swamp**
quaternary, **four**
queasy, **nausea**
qued, **evil**
quede, **evil**
quellable, **suppression**
quercine, **oak**
querimonious, **complaint**
quernal, **oak**
querulent, **complaint**
querulous, **complaint, suspicion**
questionable, **inquiry**
questioning, **implication**
quick, **rapidity**
quiescent, **peace**
quietsome, **tranquillity**
quinary, **five**
quindecennial, **year**
quinquagesimal, **fifty**
quinquecentennial, **year**
quinquennial, **year**
quinquepartite, **five**
quixotic, **behavior, romanticism**
quixotical, **behavior**
quodlibetic, **debate**
quotidian, **day**

R

rabble, **disorder, vulgarity**
Rabelaisian, **humor**
rabic, **hydrophobia**

rabid, **hydrophobia**
rabietic, **hydrophobia**
rabific, **hydrophobia**
rabiform, **hydrophobia**
rabitic, **hydrophobia**
rabulistic, **railing**
rabulous, **behavior, railing**
rachidial, **backbone**
rachidian, **backbone**
rachidiform, **backbone**
rachiform, **spine**
rachitic, **rickets**
radiant, **brightness**
radical, **root**
radicicolous, **root**
radicose, **root**
radicular, **root**
radiculose, **root**
radiographic, **x ray**
radiographical, **x ray**
radiologic, **x ray**
radiological, **x ray**
raduliform, **rasp, scraper**
raffish, **disorder, vulgarity**
rafty, **dampness**
raggy, **vexation**
raguly, **notch**
raiiform, **skate**
raisonné, **logic**
ralliform, **moor hen**
ralline, **moor hen**
ramage, **wildness**
ramal, **barb**
rameous, **barb**
ramiform, **branch**
rammish, **lust**
ramose, **branch**
ramous, **branch**
rampacious, **violence**
rampageous, **violence**
rampish, **immodesty**
ramular, **branch**
ramulose, **branch**
ranarian, **frog**
rancid, **decomposition**
rancorous, **hatred**
random, **chance**
ranine, **frog**
ranunculaceous, **buttercup**

repudiable, **discard**
rescissory, **annulment, revocation**
residual, **remainder**
residuary, **remainder**
resinaceous, **gum, lac**
resinic, **gum, lac**
resinoid, **gum, lac**
resinous, **lac, gum**
resipiscent, **reformation**
resolvent, **dissolving**
resonant, **reflection**
restiform, **cord**
retiary, **net, web**
reticulate, **net, network, web**
retiform, **net, web**
retral, **back, posterior**
retrograde, **return, reversal**
retrogressive, **reversal**
retromingent, **urination**
retroocular, **eye**
revenant, **recurrence**
reverbatory, **reflection**
reverberant, **echo, reflection**
reverberative, **echo, reflection**
reverberatory, **reflection**
rhabdoid, **rod**
rhabdomantic, **dowsing, water**
rhadamanthine, **justice**
rhagadiform, **break, crack, fissure**
rhamnaceous, **buckthorn**
rhamphoid, **beak**
rhematic, **word**
rheometric, **measurement, galva-nometer**
rhetorical, **speaker**
rhigotic, **cold**
rhinal, **nose**
rhinogenous, **nose**
rhinologic, **nose**
rhinological, **nose**
rhinorrhagic, **nosebleed**
rhizoid, **root**
rhizomic, **root**
rhizomorphic, **root**
rhizomorphoid, **root**
rhizomorphous, **root**
rhizophagous, **eating, root**
rhopaloceral, **butterfly**
rhopalocerous, **butterfly**

rhynchophorous, **beak**
rhypophobic, **fear, filth**
rictal, **gape, grimace, grin**
riggy, **wrinkle**
rimate, **fissure**
rimose, **cleft, crack, crevice, rift, split**
rimous, **crack, crevice**
rimulose, **cleft, crack**
ring, **circle**
riparian, **riverbank**
ripicolous, **riverbank**
risible, **laughter**
ritual, **ceremony, devotion**
riziform, **rice**
roborant, **strength**
robustious, **roughness**
rogatory, **question, request**
roral, **dew**
roric, **dew**
rorid, **dew**
roriferous, **dew**
rorifluent, **dew**
rorqual, **whale**
rorty, **gaiety**
rosaceous, **strawberry**
roscid, **dew**
rosorial, **gnawing**
rostellate, **beak**
rostelliform, **beak**
rostrate, **beak**
rostrated, **beak**
rostriferous, **beak**
rostriform, **beak**
rotal, **wheel**
rotiform, **wheel**
rounceval, **giant**
roupy, **hoarseness**
rubedinous, **redness**
rubefacient, **redness**
rubeolar, **measles**
rubescent, **redness**
rubicund, **redness, ruddiness**
rubiginous, **rust**
rubineous, **redness**
rubious, **redness**
rubricate, **redness**
rubricistic, **ritual**
rubricose, **redness**

S

sammy, **clamminess**
sample, **illustration**
Samsonic, **strength**
Samsonistic, **strength**
sanable, **cure, healing**
sanative, **cure, healing**
sanatory, **cure, healing**
sanct, **holiness**
sanctified, **holiness**
sanctionary, **decree**
sanctionative, **decree**
sandaliform, **slipper**
sane, **lucidity, rationality**
sanglant, **bleeding**
sanguicolous, **blood**
sanguimotor, **blood, circulation**
sanguinaceous, **blood**
sanguinary, **blood**
sanguine, **blood, optimism, redness**
sanguineous, **blood**
sanguinicolous, **blood**
sanguinivorous, **blood**
sanguinolent, **blood**
sanguinopurulent, **blood**
sanguinous, **blood**
sanguisugous, **bloodsucker, blood-thirstiness**
sanguivorous, **blood**
sanidinic, **feldspar**
sanitary, **health**
sans-culottic, **revolution**
sapid, **flavor, taste**
sapient, **knowledge, sagacity, wisdom**
sapiential, **knowledge, sagacity, wisdom**
saponaceous, **evasion, personality, soap**
saponary, **soap**
saponifiable, **soap**
saporific, **taste**
saporous, **flavor, taste**
sapphic, **erotica, verse, homosexuality**
sapphire, **blueness, corundum**
sapphiric, **corundum**
sapphirine, **blueness**
saprogenic, **decay**
saprogenous, **decay**

sapropelic, **decay, mud**
Saracenic, **nomad**
sarcastic, **taunting**
sarcastical, **taunting**
sarcodic, **protoplasm**
sarcoid, **flesh**
sarcoline, **flesh**
sarcomatoid, **tumor**
sarcomatous, **tumor**
sarcophagal, **carnivore**
sarcophagic, **animal**
sarcophagous, **animal, carnivore, flesh**
sarcophilous, **animal, carnivore, flesh**
sarcotic, **flesh**
sarcous, **flesh, muscle**
sardonic, **bitterness, linen, scorn**
sarkit, **shirt**
sarmentose, **cutting**
sartorial, **garment, tailor**
sartorian, **tailor**
satanic, **devil**
satcheled, **bag**
satient, **gratification**
satiric, **cutting, humor, irony**
satirical, **cutting, irony**
satisfactional, **fulfillment**
satisfactive, **fulfillment**
satisfactory, **amendment**
satisfied, **gratification**
satisfying, **contentment**
satrapal, **prince, tyranny**
satrapic, **prince, tyranny**
satrapical, **prince, tyranny**
saturant, **impregnation**
saturated, **absorption**
Saturnalian, **orgy, revel**
saturnine, **gloom**
satyrine, **pristineness**
saucy, **boldness, forwardness**
sauté, **frying**
sauveolent, **sweetness**
savored, **smell**
savory, **smell, taste**
saxicoline, **rock**
saxicolous, **rock**
saxifragous, **dissolution**
saxigenous, **rock**
scabbed, **scale**

scribblative, **writing**
scribblatory, **writing**
scribbled, **writing**
scriggly, **curlicue, wriggle**
scriptitory, **writing**
scriptorial, **writing**
scriptory, **writing**
scriptural, **writing**
scrolar, **parchment**
scrotiform, **pouch**
scrupular, **qualm**
scrupulous, **qualm**
scrutable, **examination**
scrutinous, **examination, search**
scullery, **kitchen**
scurrilous, **criticism**
scutal, **shield**
scutate, **shield**
scutatiform, **shield**
scutiform, **shield**
scyphate, **cup**
scyphiform, **cup, goblet**
scytodepsic, **tanning**
seathy, **danger**
sebaceous, **fat, tallow**
sebiferous, **fat**
sebific, **fat**
sec, **dryness**
secernment, **secretion**
secluded, **exclusion, isolation**
seclusive, **exclusion, isolation**
secodont, **tooth**
secret, **concealment, hiding, reticence**
secretarial, **clerk**
secretional, **emission**
secretionary, **emission**
secretitious, **emission**
secretive, **concealment, hiding, reticence**
sectorial, **tooth**
segetal, **grain**
segreant, **wing**
seignorial, **manor**
seismic, **earthquake**
seismographic, **earthquake**
seismographical, **earthquake**
seismologic, **earthquake**
seismological isoseismic, **earthquake**

selenographic, **moon**
selenographical, **moon**
selenolatrous, **moon**
selenological, **moon**
seleuomantic, **moon**
self-effacing, **reserve**
sellate, **saddle**
semantic, **meaning, word**
semasiological, **word**
sematic, **warning**
semeiologic, **meaning, word**
semeiological, **word**
semeiotic, **sign**
semeiotical, **sign**
semicentenary, **year**
semicentennial, **year**
seminiferous, **seed, semen**
seminific, **seed, semen**
seminivorous, **eating, seed**
semiologic, **sign**
semiological, **sign**
semiotic, **sign, symbol**
semiotical, **sign**
sempervirent, **evergreen**
sempervirid, **evergreen**
sempiternal, **eternity, immortality**
senary, **six**
senescent, **age, aging**
senicide, **killing, man**
senile, **aging, infirmity**
sensible, **cognizance, perception, rationality**
sententious, **aphorism**
sentient, **consciousness**
sepiid, **cuttlefish**
septenary, **seven, year**
septennial, **year**
septic, **contamination, infection**
septimal, **seven**
septuple, **seven**
septuplicate, **seven**
sepulchral, **burial, tomb**
sequacious, **behavior, imitation**
sequestral, **seclusion**
seraphic, **purity, angel**
seraphical, **angel**
seraphistic, **behavior**
serendipitous, **accident, chance**
serial, **rank, row**

sigillative, **seal**
sigillistic, **seal**
sigillographical, **seal**
sigmoid, **C, S**
sigmoidal, **C, S**
siliceous, **mineral**
sillographic, **satire, seal**
silurid, **catfish**
siluroid, **catfish**
silvan, **forest**
simian, **ape, monkey**
simiid, **chimpanzee, gibbon, gorilla, orangutan**
simious, **ape**
simple, **ease, innocence, naivety, unsophistication**
sincipital, **forehead**
sindological, **shroud**
single, **one, oneness, solitude**
singular, **one, oneness**
Sinological, **China**
sinuate, **bend, curve**
sinuous, **bend, curve, twist**
sirenic, **allure, attraction, deception, fascination**
sirenical, **allure, attraction, deception, fascination**
Sisyphean, **labor**
Sisyphian, **labor**
sittine, **nuthatch**
situal, **location**
skeigh, **shyness**
skiagraphic, **shadow**
skiagraphical, **drawing**
skiapodous, **feet**
skillful, **ingenuity**
sloe, **bluish black, purplish black**
sloped, **acclivity, declination, inclination**
sloppy, **mess**
sloth, **laziness**
slothful, **haste**
slovenly, **disorder, loafer, mess**
slow, **haste, lingering**
slubbering, **stain**
slubbery, **stain**
slug, **lingering**
sluggish, **haste, lingering**
sluicy, **flood**

sluicy, **lock**
slumbering, **sleep**
slumberous, **sleep**
smaragdine, **emerald**
smart, **acute, cleverness, competence**
smarty, **acute, cleverness**
smectic, **cleaner**
smutty, **indecency, obscenity**
snobbish, **disdain**
snuffy, **wick**
soarable, **flight**
solanaceous, **eggplant, petunia, potato**
solar, **sun**
sole, **desolation, isolation, loneliness**
solecistic, **error, grammar, syntax**
solecistical, **error**
soleiform, **slipper**
solemn, **formality, importance, seriousness**
solenoglyhic, **rattlesnake**
solenoglyphic, **viper**
solert, **skill**
soliform, **sun**
solitary, **desolation, isolation, loneliness**
solivagant, **wandering**
solivagous, **wandering**
Solonian, **wisdom**
Solonic, **wisdom**
solvent, **dissolving**
somatic, **body**
somatologic, **body**
somatological, **body**
somatosplanchnic, **body, viscera**
somatotonic, **aggressiveness, alertness, vigor**
somnambulant, **sleepwalking**
somnambulistic, **sleepwalking**
somnial, **dream, sleep**
somniative, **sleep**
somnifacient, **sleep**
somniferous, **sleep**
somnific, **sleep**
somnify, **sleep**
somniloquent, **sleep**
somnolent, **sleep**
sonal, **sound**

T

U

V

vacuolar, **cavity**
vacuous, **emptiness, void**
vacuum, **suction**
vadose, **water table**
vagabond, **wanderer**
vagarious, **wandering**
vaginal, **sheath**
vaginate, **sheath**
vaginiferous, **capsule, spore**
vainglorious, **pride**
vajra, **diamond**
valedictory, **departure, farewell, leavetaking**
valetudinaire, **invalid**
valetudinarian, **health, invalid, sickness**
valetudinary, **invalid**
valgoid, **bowlegs**
valiant, **bravery, courage**
valid, **truth**
validatory, **truth**
Valkyrian, **battle**
vallate, **rim**
vallecular, **crevice, furrow, groove**
valleculate, **crevice, furrow, groove**
valorous, **bravery, courage, intrepidity**
valuable, **worth**
valued, **esteem**
valval, **gate**
valvate, **gate**
valviferous, **gate**
valvular, **gate**
vambraced, **armor**
vandalish, **destruction**
vandalistic, **destruction**
Vandemonian, **violence**
vaned, **weathercock**
vanishing, **disappearance**
vapid, **dullness, pointlessness**
vaporable, **gas**
vapored, **gas**
vaporescence, **gas**
vaporiferous, **gas**
vaporing, **gas**
vaporish, **gas**
vapory, **gas**
Varangian, **Northman**
varanid, **monitor lizard**

vareheaded, **head**
variable, **change**
variant, **change**
variate, **diversification**
variational, **diversification**
variative, **diversification**
varicellar, **chicken pox**
varicellate, **ridge**
varicelliform, **chicken pox**
varicelloid, **chicken pox**
variciform, **dilatation**
varicoid, **dilatation**
varicolored, **diversity**
varicolorous, **diversity**
varicose, **enlargement, swelling**
varicosed, **enlargement, swelling**
varicosity, **dilatation, enlargement, swelling**
varied, **change, diversification**
varietal, **diversification**
variolate, **smallpox**
varioliform, **smallpox**
variolitic, **speck**
varioloid, **smallpox**
variolous, **smallpox**
various, **diversification**
Varsovian, **Warsaw**
varved, **stratification**
vascular, **ardor, blood vessel, vein, vessel, vigor**
vasculiform, **flowerpot**
vasculolymphatic, **blood vessel**
vasculose, **blood vessel**
vasiferous, **duct, vessel**
vasiform, **duct, tube, vessel**
vassaled, **servility**
vatic, **oracle, prophecy, prophet**
vatical, **prophecy**
vaticidal, **killing, prophet**
vaticinal, **prophecy**
vaticinatory, **prophecy**
Vedic, **Aryan**
vegetational, **plant**
vegetative, **plant**
vehemency, **force**
vehiculary, **transportation**
vehiculatory, **transportation**
veiled, **disguise**
veined, **variegation**

veinous, **variegation**
veiny, **variegation**
velamentous, **sail**
velar, **palate**
velaric, **palate**
velate, **veil**
velic, **sail**
veliferous, **sail**
veliform, **palate**
veligerous, **mollusk**
vellicative, **twitch**
vellumy, **parchment**
velocious, **quickness, speed**
velocitous, **quickness, speed**
velutinous, **velvet**
venal, **bribery, corruption, purchase**
venatic, **hunting**
venatical, **hunting**
venational, **hunting**
venatorial, **hunting**
vendible, **sale, selling**
Venedotian, **Wales**
veneficious, **sorcery**
venenate, **poison, sorcery**
venene, **sorcery**
venenose, **poison**
venerable, **respect**
venerant, **reverence**
venerate, **reverence**
venerative, **reverence**
venereal, **aphrodisiac, genitals, in-tercourse**
venerean, **Venus**
venerian, **Venus**
veneriform, **quahog**
Venetian, **Venice**
vengeful, **vendetta**
venial, **excuse, pardon**
veninific, **venom**
venison, **deer**
venomous, **poison**
venose, **vein**
venous, **vein**
vental, **wind**
ventilate, **circulation**
ventilative, **circulation**
ventose, **flatulence**
ventral, **belly, underside**
ventral ventripotent, **abdomen**

ventric, **belly**
ventricose, **belly, bulge**
ventricular, **heart, stomach**
ventriculose, **belly**
ventripotent, **abdomen, belly**
venturous, **boldness, daring**
venulose, **vein**
venulous, **vein**
venust, **beauty, elegance**
veracious, **accuracy, genuine, preci-sion, truth**
verandaed, **portico**
verbal, **conveyance**
verbatim, **reproduction**
verberative, **flogging**
verbigerative, **repetition**
verbomotor, **speech**
verbose, **talkativeness, wordiness**
verboten, **prohibition**
verdant, **greenness**
verdazure, **bluish green**
verdazurine, **bluish green**
verdigrisy, **greenness**
verdured, **greenness**
verecund, **bashfulness, modesty**
vergent, **end**
vericulate, **tuft**
veridical, **genuine, reality, truth**
veridicous, **genuine**
verifiable, **confirmation, proof**
verificative, **confirmation**
verisimilar, **truth**
verisimilitudinous, **truth**
veritable, **truth**
vermian, **worm**
vermicious, **worm**
vermicular, **worm**
vermiculated, **worm**
vermiculose, **worm**
vermiform, **worm**
vermilion, **redness**
verminal, **worm**
vermiphobic, **fear, worm**
vermorel, **nozzle**
vernacular, **native**
vernal, **spring**
vernant, **flourish, spring**
vernicose, **gleam, polish, shine**
vernile, **servility**

Index

Index

W

waddy, **tuft**
wafery, **thinness**
waggish, **joker, wit**
waggly, **unsteadiness**
wailful, **grief, lamentation**
wailsome, **lamentation**
wakeful, **vigilance**
walled, **fortification**
wan, **pallor**
warm-blooded, **fervency, irascibility**
warmhearted, **generosity, kindness**
waspish, **irascibility**
waspy, **irascibility**
wayward, **disobedience**
wearisome, **dullness**
Welsh, **Wales**
Wertherian, **sentimentality**
western, **Occident**
whelked, **twist**
whole-hearted, **devotion, sincerity**
whole-souled, **devotion**
wineglass, **hull**
wishy-washy, **insipidness**
wried, **contortion, diversion**
writhen, **contortion, twist**
Wykehamical, **Winchester College**
Wykehamist, **Winchester College**

X

xanthic, **yellowness**
xanthodermic, **race**
xanthomelanous, **blackness**
xanthotrichous, **blandness**
xanthous, **blandness, yellowness**
xenarthral, **armadillo, sloth**
xenial, **hospitality**
xenogamous, **fertilization**
xenomorphic, **form**
xenomorphous, **form**
Xenophanean, **pantheism**

xenophobic, **fear, foreigner, hatred**
xenthral, **ground sloth**
xeric, **deficiency, dryness**
xerocole, **tolerance**
xerophilic, **drought**
xerophilous, **desert, drought**
xerophobic, **desert, drought, dryness, fear**
xerophobous, **drought**
xerothermic, **aridness**
xerotic, **dryness**
xiphioid, **swordfish**
xiphoid, **sword**
xylary, **wood**
xylographic, **carving, engraving**
xylographical, **carving, engraving**
xyloid, **carving, wood**
xylomantic, **divination**
xylophagous, **eating, wood**

Y

yahwistic, **God**
yankee, **shrewdness**
yappy, **chatter**
yeomanly, **attendant**
yieldable, **submission**
yielding, **submission**
youthful, **child**
youthly, **child**
ypsiliform, **Y**

Z

zealotic, **fanaticism**
zealous, **eagerness**
Zendaic, **magic**
zenith, **pinnacle**
zenithal, **pinnacle**
Zenographic, **Jupiter**
zenographical, **Jupiter**

Index